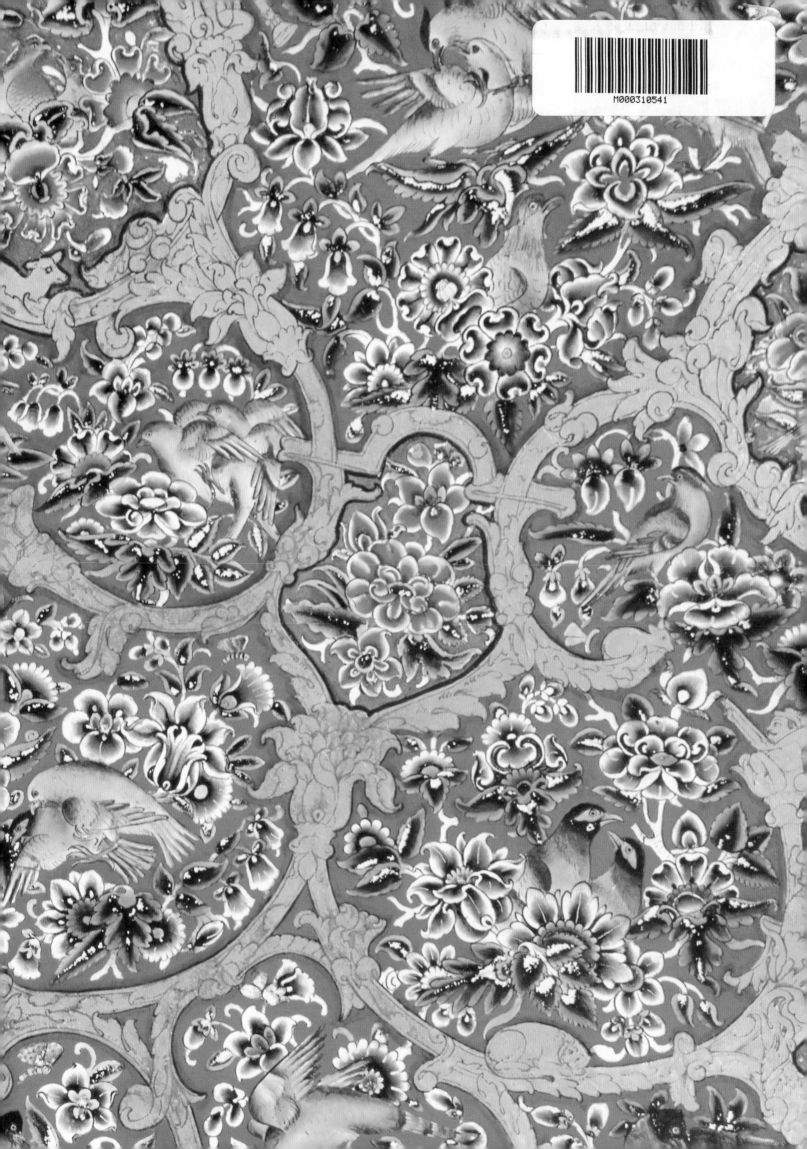

INDIA SUBLIME

PRINCELY PALACE HOTELS OF RAJASTHAN

INDIA SUBLIME

PRINCELY PALACE HOTELS OF RAJASTHAN

PHOTOGRAPHY BY MELBA LEVICK

TEXT BY MITCHELL SHELBY CRITES AND AMEETA NANJI

RIZZOLI
NEW YORK

First published in the United States of America in 2007 by
RIZZOLI INTERNATIONAL PUBLICATIONS, INC.
300 Park Avenue South, New York, NY 10010
www.rizzoliusa.com

ISBN-10: 0-8478-2979-0
ISBN-13: 978-0-8478-2979-8
LCCN: 2007924266

Designed by ABIGAIL STURGES

Printed and bound in China

2007 2008 2009 2010 2011/ 10 9 8 7 6 5 4 3 2 1

ENDPAPER *The eighteenth-century paintings inside the Chamber
of Gold at Kuchaman Fort reflect a delightful fusion of Persian,
Mughal, and Rajput styles. Adorning the walls are courting birds
framed by gilded floral arabesques in which forest creatures lie
camouflaged by the ornamental scrolling pattern.*

PAGE 1 *Detail of a carved column from one of the palace
bedrooms at Samode Haveli in Jaipur. The columns are painted
with scrolling flowers and set with cut pieces of mirror.*

PAGES 2–3 *Exterior pools and water channels at Udaivilas
in Udaipur.*

Contents

Introduction

One state alone, Rajasthan, obsessed me and drew me back. What drew me back … the taste of the mango fruit, the beauty of the white lotus, the screeching of peacocks…. In every temple of white marble or golden alabaster, I found jasmine and marigold, sandalwood and honey ritualistically offered to the gods. The myriad royal palaces and fortresses were often derelict, mere ghosts of a splendor, rivalling the ornate courts of Europe's Golden Age.

—Roloff Beny

Invading armies, caravans of merchants, itinerant holy men, artists, and poets in search of a new life in a foreign land have for millennia crossed the vast Thar Desert into Rajasthan, the legendary Land of Kings. Some were victorious in battle; some suffered crushing defeat. Others made or lost fortunes and rose to positions of fame and power. All were dazzled and astounded by the magnificent architecture and sumptuous, often sublime, decoration of the castles, forts, gardens, and palaces created by the hereditary rulers of Rajasthan.

When the gifted Canadian photographer Roloff Beny first explored Rajasthan nearly fifty years ago, these extraordinary buildings were virtually inaccessible to the public, insulated as the private domain of hereditary rulers. Many of the earliest structures lay abandoned and crumbling. Since then, however, much has changed, and the new caravans of visitors flocking to Rajasthan are now able to encounter and experience the magic and mystery of royal life at first hand. More than one hundred ancestral properties, ranging from small courtyard mansions to majestic fortresses and palaces, have been converted into elegant heritage hotels, and more are opening every day. *India Sublime* explores twenty-one of these remarkable princely estates, which incorporate within their walls

PRECEDING PAGES
PAGE 6 *A stylized marble fountain carved in the shape of a lotus and filled with rose petals stands in the center of an octagonal reception area at Udaivilas. The walls are decorated with mirrored flowering plants, a favorite decorative motif found in many Udaipur palaces.*

PAGE 7 *Virtually every inch of the grand darbar hall at Samode Palace is painted, gilded, or mirrored with scrolling floral and geometric motifs. The upper story of the hall served as the zenana apartments, where ladies of the court could view the banquets and rituals taking place below.*

more than a thousand years of creative design and decoration inspired by both East and West.

The legendary lifestyle of the maharajas and hereditary rulers was grand and luxurious. No expense was spared in the magnificent decoration of their palaces. They had at their command the finest master artisans and artists, stone carvers, and textile weavers of the age. When the Mongol conqueror Timur sacked Delhi in 1398, he took back to Central Asia not only caravans of elephants and camels loaded with precious jewels and gold, but also the "living treasures" of India as he called them, thousands of gifted artisans. These artisans were put to work embellishing his magnificent capital cities of Samarkand and Bukhara; six centuries later, their descendants still live in Central Asia, practicing their traditional arts.

The stylistic diversity and complexity of art, architecture, and decoration found in Rajasthan are directly related to the long and tumultuous history of the region. Archaeological excavations have revealed that Rajasthan was an integral part of the pre-Aryan Indus Valley civilization, a remarkable and highly sophisticated political system that flourished in the second and third millennia B.C., with strong cultural and trade connections reaching as far westward as Mesopotamia.

Around 1500 B.C., Indo-Aryan tribes began to move into northwestern India from Central Asia through the Hindu Kush mountain range. They brought with them a new language, Sanskrit, and worshiped a previously unknown pantheon of gods whose roles and rituals were described in the *Rig Veda*, one of the earliest religious texts known. Out of this Vedic cauldron emerged three great religions—Jainism, Buddhism, and Hinduism—which spread across large parts of Asia.

Contact with Greek civilization came through Alexander the Great, who reached the banks of the Indus River in 327 B.C. before returning home with the remnants of his exhausted troops. The imperial rule of the Mauryas in the third century B.C., and the Guptas five centuries later, brought peace and stability to Rajasthan as well as major cultural achievements in the fields of art, architecture, philosophy, and literature.

The Golden Age of the Guptas was shattered by the repeated invasions of the Huns, tribal nomads from the steppes of Central Asia, whose devastating incursions into northern India hastened the fall of the empire. During the sixth or seventh century A.D., a number of nomadic warring tribes entered central and western India following in the wake of the Hun armies.

FACING PAGE *Meandering water channels flow in and around the buildings of Udaivilas, providing a natural source of air conditioning and the soothing sound of gently splashing water in the corridors.*

ABOVE *Covered by an embroidered canopy, a traditional cushioned swing is available for the relaxation of the guests at Bhanwar Niwas, Bikaner.*

These tightly knit clans of *kshatriya*, or hereditary warriors, traced their dynastic origins back to the sun (*surya*), moon (*chandra*), and fire (*agni*). Historians today feel that they are probably the ancestors of the modern-day Rajputs, or sons of kings, who became the hereditary rulers of Rajasthan.

The fabled riches of Hindu temples and the wealth of the maharajas continued to tempt armies and raiding parties from Afghanistan and Persia. From the tenth century onward, the Rajput rulers began to construct massive fortified citadels, which were entered through monumental gateways and often surrounded by deep moats filled with water. Crenellated walls punctuated by narrow arrow slits and broad ramparts crowned by *chhatris*, or domed towers, became the defining features of early Rajput fort architecture. Protected by the outer walls of the town, wealthy merchants built imposing *havelis*, large and often elaborately decorated mansions arranged around interior courtyards.

Royal palaces were normally located within an inner fortification perched high on a hilltop or at the end of a narrow valley. They were traditionally arranged around a series of square or rectangular courtyards and were strictly divided into public and private areas.

The royal apartments and the *zenana*, where the queens and ladies of the court resided, were kept separate from the main palace and were located in the most secure part of the palace complex.

As a consequence of the constant fighting and defense of their borders, the Rajput warriors developed a medieval code of chivalry. To avoid the shame of capture in the event that their husbands were defeated in battle, the warriors' brave wives would throw themselves on the funeral pyre in the ritual of *sati*. These heroic events, immortalized in poetry and folk ballads, are still narrated and sung by itinerant minstrels throughout Rajasthan:

And he fought a great and famous battle
and passed to heaven, a god among chieftains.
His wife, loyal and loving, beloved and fair,
followed close behind him into the flames.

In 1192, large parts of northern India finally fell to Afghan invaders led by Muhammad Ghuri, who defeated the great Rajput king Prithviraj Chauhan at the battle of Tarain near Delhi. This momentous battle ushered in a period of central-

ized Muslim rule under the Delhi sultanate, which continued uninterrupted until the arrival of Babur, the first Mughal emperor, who wrested power from the sultans in 1526. After many heroic military campaigns and sieges, the majority of the Rajput kingdoms succumbed. As long as they acknowledged the allegiance of the imperial authority based in Delhi and Agra, they were allowed to keep their kingdoms intact. In some Rajput states, such as Jaipur, intermarriage with the Mughals was common, and the maharajas and nobles there rose to positions of great power and influence in the Mughal army and court, serving as trusted generals and ministers of state throughout the empire.

The Mughals brought a certain degree of peace, stability, and prosperity to large areas of India. It was during this time that the maharajas began to expand their palaces, adding large *darbar* halls for public and private receptions, sumptuous throne rooms, royal apartments, and formal gardens laid out with ornamental pools, water channels, and elegant domed pavilions of pleasure. Inspired directly by the magnificent Mughal architecture of Delhi and Agra, new materials and techniques were adopted to embellish the exterior and interior of Rajput forts and palaces.

Wall painting using both wet and dry fresco rapidly became a standard decorative technique in the forts and palaces of Rajasthan. The original inspiration may have been Mughal, but the adaptation to local Rajput tastes and styles was creative and striking. Scrolling floral arabesques, ornate geometric patterns, narrative murals illustrating heroic epics and the tales of star-crossed lovers, equestrian studies, and portrait galleries of maharajas and their courtiers were among the most popular themes. Traditional pigments were made out of crushed semiprecious stones, minerals, and plants highlighted with pure

gold leaf. Only the finest master artisans, whose skills were passed down from father to son, were commissioned to design and execute the intricate painting for the royal throne room and principal apartments.

The use of thousands of small pieces of cut and faceted mirror and colored glass set in frames of gilded plaster for wall decoration probably came from Persia through the Mughals. Almost every Rajput palace had a glittering *sheesh mahal*, or palace of mirrors, which evoked glittering pools of water or a star-filled night sky. Pierced-work screens called *jalis*, intricately carved in floral and geometric patterns out of golden, beige, and red sandstone and pure white marble, gently filtered light and air throughout the palace. Occasionally, panels of colored glass were set in the fretwork, which created rainbowlike effects across the room. In the hands of a great master stone carver, *jalis* could become major works of art in their own right.

As the Mughal empire began to weaken at the beginning of the eighteenth century, the power and influence of foreign trading companies and colonial powers gradually grew stronger. The British ultimately grabbed the "jewel in the crown" in 1857, following an uprising of native states now known as the First War of Indian Independence, which ended with the exile of the last Mughal emperor, Bahadur Shah Zafar, to Rangoon. The maharajas retained their kingdoms and many privileges, although they were bound by yet another new allegiance, this time to the British Empire, whose first capital in Calcutta was shifted in 1911 to New Delhi. Neoclassical architecture, fashionable in Europe in the nineteenth century, soon became part of the colonial style of architecture as well. In the early twentieth century, experiments with art deco ornament and design in a number of palaces were especially successful.

FACING PAGE *Some of the finest wall paintings in Rajasthan are found inside the royal apartments at Kuchaman Fort. Framed within a carved and gilded arch, this delicate painting depicts a ruler deep in conversation with a courtier.*

RIGHT *Painted on the walls of Shiv Niwas Palace, a caparisoned elephant marches in procession surrounded by courtiers carrying a parasol, flag, and standard, part of the royal regalia of the Udaipur State.*

BELOW *A vase of flowers painted in French rococo style adorns one of the walls of the main dining hall at Bhanwar Niwas. The fresco was painted by the hotel's current owner, Sunil Rampura.*

FOLLOWING PAGE *The walls of the zenana at Samode Palace, located within the upper story of the darbar hall, are suitably painted with portraits and figures of the beautiful women who once lived there.*

In Rajasthan, nascent stirrings of nationalism led to the creation of magnificent new palaces and civic buildings designed in a Rajput revivalist style. Ironically, the movement was spearheaded by Sir Samuel Swinton Jacob, a scholarly British architect and chief engineer of Jaipur State, who incorporated traditional elements of Rajput architecture, such as projecting balconies known as *jharokhas*, as well as *jalis* and domed *chhatri* towers and pavilions with slanting *bangla* roofs. He was also responsible for several of the major palaces built during the early twentieth century in Rajasthan.

The efforts of the legendary Hindu leader Mahatma Gandhi, who nurtured and guided the struggle for freedom through decades of oppression and tactical negotiation, culminated in the partition and independence of India in 1947. After some initial resistance, the thousands of princely states across the country were absorbed into the fabric of modern India. As socialist India took shape, hereditary titles, lands, and privileges were gradually whittled away. Many rulers struggled to maintain their ancestral forts and palaces, and some had to part with them at throwaway prices.

With the rise of global tourism in the second half of the twentieth century, a number of princely rulers began to convert their ancestral forts and palaces into luxury hotels and resorts. That more people visit Rajasthan than any other part of India was clearly a major motivating factor. Many rulers still live in private apartments of the palace, and they regularly greet visitors and organize lavish banquets and other entertainment in a grand royal style, just as their ancestors had done before them.

In order to accommodate the constantly increasing number of domestic and international tourists, heritage hotels are being expanded with the creation of new restaurants, Ayurvedic health spas, swimming pools, and ornamental gardens. The original carved, painted, and mirrored walls of the forts and palaces are also being sensitively restored. This has brought an unexpected bonus of steady work to the many gifted artists and artisans whose ancestors originally created these remarkable buildings. The return of traditional patronage helps to ensure that these precious and endangered traditional arts are not only revived but will also be passed on to the next generation. Thus, the rich traditions and regal splendor of Rajasthan remain alive and well and, more than ever, accessible to all who visit the region.

GLOSSARY

agni	fire
Ayurveda	science of life (from ayus, "life," and veda, "knowledge")
bagh	garden
bangla	curved roof or vault derived from the thatched roofs of Bengali village huts
bazaar	market
bhawan	hall, apartment, or grand residence
brahmin	highest of the four Hindu castes, whose members traditionally would have performed priestly functions
chandra	moon
chhajja	overhanging eave or architectural sunshade
chhatri	domed pavilion or tower, often placed on the upper levels of a building
chitera	fresco painter
darbar	royal audience hall
diwan-i-am	hall of public audience
diwan-i-khas	hall of private audience
Ganesh	elephant-headed Hindu deity, the Lord of the Remover of Obstacles, who is invoked at the start of new ventures
haveli	residential mansion or complex built around one or more open courtyards
jali	ornamental pierced screen or lattice usually carved in stone or wood
Jats	non-Rajput Hindu rulers in eastern Rajasthan
jharokha	projecting window or balcony roofed with a dome or vault
Krishna	popular Hindu deity, the Lord of Love, and an incarnation of Vishnu
kshatriya	Hindu warrior caste to which many hereditary rulers belong
Lakshmi	(also spelled Laxmi), Hindu goddess of Wealth and Learning
maha	prefix meaning "'great"
mahal	palace or regal apartment
maharaja	great king
maharana	royal title for the kings of Udaipur
maharani	great queen
Marwar	Rajput kingdom (Rathore dynasty) of Jodhpur in western Rajasthan
Mewar	Rajput kingdom (Sisodia dynasty) of Udaipur in the southwestern corner of Rajasthan
Mughals	conquerers of Central Asian descent who ruled large parts of India from 1526 to 1857, basing themselves in their three principal capitals of Agra, Delhi, and Lahore
niwas	dwelling or house
pan	betel leaf containing areca nut, lime paste, and other fragrant ingredients; often chewed after a meal
pol	monumental entrance gateway
Radha	beloved of Lord Krishna
Raj	period of direct colonial rule of India by the British (1858–1947)
Rajput	warrior class of Rajasthan
rang mahal	palace of colors
rawal/rawat	hereditary titles of a landed nobility in Rajasthan
sheesh mahal	palace of mirrors
surya/Surya	the sun/Hindu sun god
thakur	hereditary title of a landed noble in Rajasthan
thikana	hereditary fiefdom within a Rajput state, the domain of a thakur or rawal
vilas	palace
zamindar	hereditary landowner
zenana	women's apartments

Neemrana Fort-Palace

NEEMRANA

The small, sleepy village of Neemrana is about 70 miles (120 kilometers) south of Delhi. To reach it requires a sudden, right turn, which can easily be missed, off the main Delhi-Jaipur Highway. About three or four miles along a narrow dirt road, through a nondescript arid landscape, past the village, a steep hill leads to the entrance into the Neemrana Fort through the grand Surya Pol (Gate of the Sun). Out of the blue appear lush orange and dusty pink bougainvillea cascading over ancient stone walls, a refreshing sight after the parched surroundings below.

Legend has it that the fierce warriors of Rajasthan, the Rajputs, did not consider themselves "born of a woman" but believed themselves to be *suryavanshi*, or direct descendants of the sun. Their pride was as legendary as their ability to fight, yet neither was enough to hold back the wave of Mughal invasions. The Rajput dynasty of the Chauhan clan, which had ruled the region from Ajmer to Delhi since the tenth century, was defeated and driven southwest. It was here in 1464, in this new Chauhan capital of Neemrana, that the reigning raja, Rajdeo, built a formidable fort palace. Situated on a grand plateau, the structure is cut into the hillside, hidden and protected in a horseshoe formation by the Aravalli mountain range. These ancient hills form a backbone running northeast for about 350 miles (563 kilometers) through the state of Rajasthan. Rajdeo's descendants inhabited the fort until 1947, when Maharaja Rajendra Singh, in the face of the abolition of his princely privileges, decided to abandon the fort and move to a more modest residence.

PRECEDING PAGES

LEFT *Neemrana Fort-Palace at sunset, showing its vast stepped buildings cut into the verdant hillside. The buildings are interspersed with luxuriant leafy trees and bougainvillea.*

RIGHT *The Chand Pol, or Gate of the Moon, forms the west entrance into Fort Neemrana, The majestic gateway, with its massive iron-spiked wooden doors, discouraged charging elephants during enemy invasions. The scalloped frame of the archway is covered with floral paintings.*

TOP AND RIGHT *Fort Neemrana's sprawling architecture and lush green surroundings can be viewed from several vantage points.*

ABOVE *A metal water pot sits in one of the fort's lookout niches, which is bordered by small arched alcoves.*

ABOVE
*A bedroom with a traditional charpai, or high bed
with red-lacquered wooden legs.*

RIGHT
*This bedroom is furnished with typical Indo-Colonial
furniture. The room's ceiling is embellished with mirrors
and carved wooden flower details.*

RIGHT *Interior courtyard with a lotus pool. Water plays a key role in Mughal and Rajput architecture. Flowing water channels, pools, and rippling fountains combine with fierce summer winds to create natural methods of air conditioning that continue to cool the air and the thick sandstone walls of the building.*

Neemrana lay abandoned and in ruins until 1986, when new owners, art historian Aman Nath and French businessman Francis Wacziarg, visualized its potential and began a four-year process of restoration, reconstruction, and transformation into a very comfortable palace hotel. Its vast stepped buildings rise to ten levels and extend across three acres of the twenty-acre property. Once inside, it is easy to lose one's way in a maze of inner and outer courtyards, stairwells, narrow corridors, pools, and fountains. At sunset, golden sunlight streams through the openwork of the *jali* windows, throwing patterned light and shadows onto thick sandstone walls.

Additions have been carried out with such skill that it is not apparent at first what actually has been added. The original interiors have been entirely reconstituted and decorated with traditional textiles and carefully chosen objects. On one of the terraces is an inviting swimming pool and spa that offers holistic Ayurvedic healing treatments. In the evenings, under the stars, you can watch renowned Indian classical musicians and dancers, like Rama Vaidyanathan, perform in the spectacular amphitheater. Inspired by music, Wacziarg has set up the Neemrana Music Foundation to encourage the performance of Western classical opera in India. The foundation has sponsored several Indian-themed operas, including Georges Bizet's *The Pearl Fishers* and fellow Frenchman Leo Manuel's *The Fakir of Benares.*

Its past splendor reawakened, Neemrana Fort-Palace overlooks groves of shrubs, wild pigs running through thickets of low-lying thorny trees, and occasional herds of roaming deer. Green parakeets with red-pink beaks swoop incessantly from balcony to turret to tree to balcony and back. Being at Neemrana is probably the closest to feeling one is part of an Indian miniature painting.

Samode Palace

SAMODE

$\mathbb{S}$amode is about 20 miles (40 kilometers) northwest of Jaipur, surrounded by fertile green fields and a ring of sharp ridges called the Aravalli hills. Samode was once a flourishing town; today it is little more than a small, impoverished village full of potholes and crumbling houses. Like so many towns and villages in India, it survives precariously through its noble historical past.

A winding cobbled road leads through a majestic arched gateway to the main entrance of the four-hundred-year-old Samode Palace. Surrounded by a grand stone fortress, the palace is constructed on three levels in a progression of courtyards. From the narrow palace balconies are dizzying views of the enormous main courtyard below, which opens out from the vast Mughal-

style arches of the Diwan-i-am, or Hall of Public Audience. Towering above one side of the palace, the weathered, dark stone walls of Samode Fort edge the top of the undulating hills. This was the Samode family's former residence, accessible in times of trouble by an underground passageway.

The *thakurs* of Samode and the state of Amber (present-day Jaipur) were of the Nathawat clan from Chomu, whose heritage can be traced back to medieval times and the fabled Rajput hero Prithviraj Singh. One of his twelve sons, Gopal Singh, was awarded Samode, which was among the wealthiest territories in the Amber kingdom at the time. The land eventually passed on within the Nathawat clan into the hands of Behari Das, a Rajput warrior in service to the Mughal court.

PRECEDING PAGES

PAGE 22 *View of Samode Palace and Samode Fort, with the Aravalli hills in the background. The entrance steps are flanked by two* champa *(frangipani) trees leading to the entrance of the palace.*

PAGE 23 *The main gateway at the foot of the hills leads into the first large courtyard, which contains extensive lush gardens.*

PAGES 24–25 *During the day, Sultan Mahal (Palace of the King) is bathed in glowing sunlight. The walls, arches, and alcoves are covered with floral frescoes and paintings of Radha and Krishna as well as royal hunt and darbar scenes.*

FACING PAGE *A highly ornamented alcove in Sultan Mahal. The far wall has been entirely inlaid with disk-shaped mirrors.*

ABOVE *Detail of a wall in Sultan Mahal. The hand-painted fresco depicts Radha and Krishna sitting in a garden surrounded by tropical foliage, accompanied by two women attendants.*

FOLLOWING PAGES *Section of the zenana. Every inch of wall and ceiling has been hand-painted with floral designs interspersed with medallions incorporating portraits of women of the court.*

LEFT *The Sheesh Mahal (Palace of Mirrors) is ornamented with disk-shaped mirrors, colored-glass mosaic, and detailed wall paintings.*

ABOVE *Detail of Sheesh Mahal showing the intricacy and refinement of the ornamentation.*

After six generations in the hands of Behari Das's descendants, Samode was surrendered to the British; in 1757, however, the British returned Samode to the Nathawat clan, whose rulers were given the title of *rawal* in gratitude for the clan's continued loyalty to the Raj.

For the first half of its existence after it was restored to the Nathawat clan, Samode was little more than a fortified stronghold in the rugged Rajput tradition. As the rawals of Samode became affluent noblemen in the court of the maharaja of Jaipur, however, it was developed into a striking example of Rajput-Mughal architecture. In the early nineteenth century, under Rawal Bairi Sal, a statesman in the court of the maharaja of Jaipur who eventually became chief minister of Jaipur and for a while wielded absolute power in the region, the palace walls were adorned with lavish paintings and mirror work. The expansion of the palace buildings begun during Bairi Sal's reign continued under his descendant Rawal Sheo Singh. The two rawals are credited with building in the middle of Samode Palace a grand audience hall with elaborately painted fresco walls, in addition to the private accommodations at the rear.

31

ABOVE An extensively painted arched corridor wraps around the zenana.

RIGHT The Blue Room joins the zenana to other sections of the palace. The walls and ceilings have been adorned with scrolling vine patterns and floral panels painted in cool blues and whites.

BELOW *A corner sitting area in one of the bedroom suites is furnished with a raw-silk upholstered daybed and a teak wood table inlaid with camel bone.*

RIGHT *The romantic atmosphere of this bedroom suite is enhanced by scalloped arches of white marble, delicate salmon-pink painted walls, and an ivory-white mosquito net that cascades from the ceiling over the bed.*

FOLLOWING PAGES *A view of the large swimming pool and various smaller pools overlooking the Aravalli hills, surrounded by champa trees and a white marble pavilion.*

All open off three courtyards arranged in a linear succession. Today, in the largest courtyard of the palace, folk and gypsy musicians and dancers perform dazzling nighttime shows under sparkling stars

In 1985 Samode's owners enlisted builders, master crafts-people, and painters to restore the property. In 1987 Samode Palace opened its gates as a heritage hotel. It is fitting that the owners, Raghvendra Singh and his brother Yadavendra Singh, are descendants of the original Nathawat family.

The hotel contains forty-two guest rooms and several special ornamented rooms: Rang Mahal, or Palace of Colors, resembles a jewel box, with gilded and painted walls and mirror-worked ceilings. Beyond this lies Sheesh Mahal, the Palace of Mirrors, with its dazzling inlays of glass and mirror work and painted friezes of royal hunts and darbar (court) scenes. The interiors have been inspired by traditional design and painting techniques using stone-ground pigments mixed with tree resin, which are known to last for hundreds of years. Still living in the village are descendants of the original court painters who continue to be involved in the restoration of the palace frescoes.

Rambagh Palace

JAIPUR

Therewas always a feeling of magic in the air at Rambagh, the fairy tale palace which was once our gracious, comfortable and happy home.

—RAJMATA GAYATRI DEVI

The first and one of the grandest of all royal palaces to be converted into a heritage property, Rambagh Palace began as a lush and secluded garden built in 1835 for the favorite handmaiden of the queen of Maharaja Sawai Ram Singh II. Because the garden was situated five miles outside the walled city of Jaipur in the middle of thick forest, later rulers added a hunting lodge where the royal family and guests could stalk black buck, wild birds, and even the occasional tiger and panther. In the early twentieth century, the original garden pavilions were replaced by a sprawling palace designed in an eclectic fusion of Mughal and Rajput styles by Sir Samuel Swinton Jacob, a British army officer and chief engineer for the state of Rajasthan. Jacob was an architect who also had a deep scholarly interest in traditional architecture, and he created a number of the grander royal residences and public buildings of Rajasthan, including the Lallgarh Palace in Bikaner.

Maharaja Sawai Man Singh II was only eleven when he acceded to the throne in 1922. In order to give him a broader and less traditional education, it was decided that the young prince should be moved from the restrictive confines of the eighteenth-century City Palace to the Rambagh, where he would be free from the machinations of palace intrigue. Man Singh ultimately decided to make the Rambagh his official

PRECEDING PAGES

LEFT *Crowned by* chhatri *towers, the palace facade is painted in tones of deep red, cream, and white. A stone staircase flanked by two ornamental carved sandstone planters leads to the raised veranda, the principal outdoor seating area for guests.*

RIGHT *Located in each corner of the arcaded veranda is a stylized lotus fountain, carved out of local marble, which provides a welcome cooling effect on hot summer days.*

LEFT AND ABOVE *Leading up to the main reception hall, an elegant formal staircase supported by monolithic beige sandstone elephants (detail above) rises out of a tiled fountain below.*

residence and further embellished the palace by adding a number of royal suites in 1931. He continued to live here throughout most of his life with his elegant wife, Maharani Gayatri Devi, a princess of Cooch Bihar, who was universally regarded as the most beautiful woman in the world. They entertained lavishly and their guests included Queen Elizabeth and Prince Philip, heads of state, the international jet set, and leading luminaries in the world of art and cinema. In 1957 Man Singh's decision to convert the palace into a heritage hotel evoked great criticism from other Rajput royal families, although it proved to be a visionary step that not only preserved the property, but also encouraged many other royal families to do the same with their own palaces and forts.

Although sadly many of the original reception rooms and suites have been altered beyond recognition, the neoclassical swimming pool, the grand formal dining room with its illuminated alabaster urns and painted ceiling, and the red and gold lacquered Oriental Room have been left relatively unchanged.

ABOVE *Arranged on the fireplace mantel inside the Suryavanshi (Sun Dynasty) Suite, a gilded clock is framed by three porcelain vases that were imported from Italy and painted by local Jaipur miniaturists with the portrait of Maharaja Madho Singh II, who ruled Jaipur from 1880 to 1922.*

RIGHT *The Suryavanshi Suite is furnished with an Italian marble fireplace flanked by portraits of Maharaja Man Singh and Maharani Gayatri Devi, who made the Rambagh their home for many years.*

RIGHT *A life-size oil painting of the legendary beauty Maharani Gayatri Devi surveys the Rajput Room, one of two elegant dining salons in the palace.*

FOLLOWING PAGES
PAGES 46–47 *Recently restored, the indoor neoclassical swimming pool, with touches of art deco decoration, originally allowed the ladies of the royal family to relax in private and sheltered from the tanning effects of the Jaipur sun.*

PAGES 48–49 *Inspired by the formal geometry of traditional Persian and Mughal gardens, the Chandni Chowk garden, located just beyond the main reception area, is divided into four sections separated by a long, tiled water channel flowing from a central sandstone fountain. Seen from above, the low, green hedge planting, meticulously clipped in the shape of interlocking eight-pointed stars, recreates the intricate patterns of a Persian carpet.*

Carved furniture, royal portraits, and works of art remain on display in many of the principal suites and reception rooms, vividly recalling the original splendor of the palace. In a major building and refurbishment program completed in 2002, an imposing new entrance gateway, reception hall, and formal garden were created. Arriving under a lofty porch resting on monolithic beige sandstone columns, guests ascend a grand staircase supported by four massive elephants carved from matching stone by local artisans. The spacious reception hall, embellished with a carved marble fountain and floors inlaid with colored stone, leads directly onto a balcony that overlooks the newly constructed Chandni Chowk garden, where the finest saffron outside of Kashmir was once cultivated by order of the maharaja himself. The majestic central fountain, geometric planting, and tiled water channels dividing the Chandni Chowk into four sections clearly draw their inspiration from the classical gardens of Persia and Mughal India. Although the most glamorous couple of their time no longer live here, the mystique and magic of their unique legacy continues to enthrall all those who come.

Alsisar Haveli

JAIPUR

Located just outside the walled city of Jaipur near the auspicious Gate of the Moon, Alsisar Haveli is one of the hidden jewels of the Pink City. Leaving the bustle of the local bazaar behind, guests enter through an elaborately carved sandstone gateway into a garden oasis scented with jasmine and cascading bougainvillea. The original rather modest haveli was built in 1892 by Thakur Ganpat Singh, who served as the Minister of Forest and Wildlife in the Jaipur State. The Alsisar family were among a number of thakurs who owed direct allegiance to the maharaja of Jaipur. The ancestral *thikana*, or fiefdom, of Alsisar is located 120 miles (193 kilometers) north of Jaipur in the historic region of Shekhawati, which was once the crossroads for merchant caravans arriving on the Silk Road from Central Asia and China.

The current thakur of Alsisar, Gaj Singh, and his wife, Thakurani Manju Singh, decided to convert their ancestral property into a heritage hotel in 1992. They have greatly enlarged the existing core building by adding a tiled swimming pool, forty-seven rooms, and a magnificent two-story dining hall supported by carved marble columns. A small temple dedicated to Lord Shiva stands at the edge of the raised veranda, the main outdoor sitting area of the haveli, where the daily worship of the Lord of Creation has gone on uninterrupted for more than a century.

An expert on conservation and restoration of heritage properties, Gaj Singh both designs and supervises the work done by his team of master carvers, artisans, painters, and specialists in glass and mirror work. The dining hall, reception foyer,

PRECEDING PAGES
LEFT *Articulated with carved red sandstone
railings and jharokha balconies, the two-story
entrance to the haveli, with its beige plastered
walls, was built in traditional Rajput style at
the beginning of the twentieth century.*

RIGHT *Supported by monumental white marble
columns, the elegant central dining hall represents
traditional Rajasthani style. It was designed and
built by the owner in 2004.*

ABOVE AND RIGHT *Delicate foliate patterns
painted by master Jaipur artists with pure gold
leaf and stone-ground colors embellish the
arched walls of the dining hall.*

and many of the guest rooms at Alsisar Haveli are finely decorated with floral arabesques painted with traditional stone-
ground colors, accented by touches of gold leaf and inset with
colored glass and glittering mirror work. Local carpenters have
carved the period furniture and beds for the rooms, which
are decorated and draped with traditional block-printed
Rajasthani cotton fabric.

As part of a growing trend of hoteliers in Rajasthan to
expand into other areas of the state, Gaj Singh has constructed
two new palace hotels designed in traditional Rajput style.
Nahargarh, surrounded by a twenty-foot-high stone fortress, is
brilliantly situated on the borders of the famous tiger sanctuary of Ranthambhor.

53

PRECEDING PAGES *Accented by handmade mirror cut into geometric shapes, the upper stained-glass windows of the main salon are designed in the shape of a half-lotus set with vivid primary colors.*

LEFT *The spacious bedrooms are furnished with locally made block-printed curtains and bedcovers, glittering glass chandeliers, and baroque wooden furniture.*

ABOVE *Colored-glass panels above the windows and doors of the guest rooms illustrate stories associated with Lord Krishna, seen here during Holi, the Festival of Color, in a lotus pool surrounded by his gopis, or female devotees.*

The second, Amar Mahal, stands on the banks of the Betwa River, near the small temple town of Orchha in the central Indian state of Madhya Pradesh, which shares a border with Rajasthan. Gaj Singh has also personally overseen a major and masterful renovation at Alsisar Mahal, the family's ancestral fortified palace, which was virtually a ruin.

Thakur Gaj Singh and other owners of heritage properties across Rajasthan have in a significant way promoted a major revival of traditional Rajasthani arts and crafts through their extensive renovation and building programs. Continued patronage on such a scale, coupled with their insistence on the highest quality of craftsmanship, will help ensure that these precious artistic traditions will never disappear.

ABOVE *Guests enter the hotel through lush gardens shaded by tall neem trees and scented with trailing white jasmine.*

RIGHT *The elegant arched arcades of the inner courtyard formed the core of the original haveli.*

FOLLOWING PAGES *Four sandstone pavilions covered with typical sloping roofs, called* bangla, *frame the tiled swimming pool, which features a leaping blue dolphin in the center.*

Narain Niwas Palace

JAIPUR

The thakurs of Kanota, whose ancestral state is located only 20 miles (32 kilometers) outside of Jaipur on the Agra road, rose to positions of considerable power in the Jaipur court from the end of the nineteenth century until the independence of India in 1947. Like many other noble families of the time, they required a suitably grand residence in Jaipur.

Surrounded by high walls and entered through an imposing painted gateway, the original hunting lodge located near the Rambagh palace gardens was created by thakur Narain Singh at the end of the nineteenth century and became known locally as Narain Niwas. His son, General Amar Singh, who served as Commander of Forces for Jaipur State, decided in 1924 to construct a much grander palace, which

became his principal Jaipur residence until his death in 1942. He became personally involved in the design, which drew its inspiration from traditional Rajput architecture but was distinguished by its brightly colored yellow and red walls painted with a variety of floral and naturalistic designs.

While serving in a number of powerful positions in the military and administration of Jaipur State, Amar Singh also found time to write the longest diary in the world. Writing in English over a forty-year period, he recorded in intimate detail the activities of Jaipur court and daily life. Perhaps inspired by the diary, his grandson, thakur Mohan Singh, converted the ancestral home into a heritage hotel in 1978.

PRECEDING PAGES
PAGE 62 *Bright primary colors with a dash of Jaipur pink thrown in add an exuberant vitality to the veranda walls.*

PAGE 63 *The same rainbow colors, reminiscent of tie-and-dyed turbans, are ingeniously applied to the interior columns and walls.*

PAGES 64–65 *The former darbar hall, an exotic blend of European and Rajput styles, has been converted into the main interior sitting area for the hotel. Carved wooden furniture, paintings of ancestors on horseback, and family mementos and curios in the glass cabinets lend a feeling of traditional grandeur to the room.*

ABOVE AND RIGHT *Afternoon light streams through the colored-glass windows of the main dining hall.*

ABOVE *Leading from the ceremonial entrance gateway to the main palace beyond, the broad welcoming driveway is carpeted with orange marigold flowers and guarded by a pair of antique cannon.*

FACING PAGE *Festooned with flower garlands, the colorfully painted terrace is the central gathering point for guests.*

FOLLOWING PAGES *The four principal suites are elegantly furnished with four-poster beds draped with local block-printed fabric, carved period furniture, and crystal chandeliers.*

He wisely retained much of the original furniture, works of art, arms and armor, antique photographs, and ancestral paintings, which add an aura of traditional Rajput splendor to the property. Mohan Singh's sons now look after Narain Niwas and can often be found sitting on the broad veranda porch, where, just as their father had done before them, they continue to entertain and regale the guests with legends and stories of bygone days.

The transformation of an old pavilion in the garden known as the Rang Mahal, or Palace of Color, into a popular bar and

barbecue has been a brilliant success and is filled with hotel guests and Jaipur locals every evening. The extensive palace gardens, which house at the far end of the property a bustling nursery filled with exotic plants and trees, are slowly being restored to their original grandeur. Peacocks seem to love the Narain Niwas gardens, and there are more here than anywhere else in Jaipur. They strut, preen, and screech, and, when chased by the palace pet beagle, fly clumsily upward, escaping to the nearest branch. Fortunately, things change slowly in Jaipur.

Samode Haveli

JAIPUR

Samode Haveli, perhaps the most sumptuously and richly decorated of all the heritage hotels of Jaipur, is located near Zorawar Singh Gate, just outside the city walls and just over the hill from Amber, the ancestral capital of Jaipur. The haveli was constructed in the second half of the nineteenth century by Rawal Bairi Sal to serve as his Jaipur town house. Rawal Bairi, who served for a number of years as prime minister of Jaipur state, not only had the resources but also the passion for building in a grand style, as his ancestral palace and garden at Samode, built about twenty years earlier, clearly show (see page 22).

Samode Haveli has gone through a series of significant face-lifts in recent years. Guests who stayed in what was a rather sleepy, laid-back hotel in the 1980s still warmly recall being asked to leave the hotel for a couple of hours while a goat was sacrificed in the central courtyard to propitiate the gods and assure the good fortune of the ruling family. That same grassy courtyard has now become one of the most elegant places to dine on a Jaipur evening. Tables are arranged around marble fountains planted with white lotus and illuminated by twinkling fairy lights hanging from the branches of pomegranate and orange trees. The food is refined and varied. Guests can choose from a delicious menu featuring traditional Rajasthani, South Indian, and Western cuisine while being serenaded by the haunting sound of desert flute and the hypnotic rhythms of gypsy castanets.

When the weather is too hot or the monsoon rains have started, the original darbar hall adjacent to the central courtyard is converted into an air-conditioned dining room.

PRECEDING PAGES

PAGE 72 *The walls and ceilings of the sumptuous Maharaja Suite, traditionally known as the Sheesh Mahal, or Palace of Mirrors, are completely covered with original gilded plaster and glittering glass mosaic.*

PAGE 73 *Every inch of the walls of this elegant suite is covered with fine painting and mirror work. In the lower panel, Lord Krishna serenades his adoring consort, Radha, with the divine music of his flute.*

PAGES 74–75 *Adjacent to the central courtyard, the reception area is framed by marble columns and furnished with comfortable cane and wood furniture.*

PAGES 76–77 *Illuminated by crystal chandeliers, the main dining hall of Samode Haveli, once the darbar, is completely painted with floral arabesques, bouquets of roses, and silver trays brimming with fruit.*

RIGHT *Tucked away in a corner of the formal dining room, this small painted alcove appears to be embraced by a garden of flowers.*

FOLLOWING PAGES *Sheltered by painted columns and a mirrored ceiling, this traditional raised platform in the Maharaja Suite is furnished with velvet cushions offering a view to the palace gardens beyond and a great place for an afternoon nap.*

Created by Rawal Sheo Singhji in the third quarter of the nineteenth century, its painted walls abound with floral arabesques, bouquets of roses, and plates of fruit and sweetmeats symbolizing the joys of banqueting and ritual celebration.

Reflecting the social hierarchy of traditional living arrangements, the rooms and suites vary from small and cozy to grand and highly decorated. The Sheesh Mahal, or Palace of Mirrors, now renamed the Maharaja Suite, has some of the finest and most delicate glass and mirror-work decoration found in Jaipur. This magical room springs to life in the evening when candles reflect every facet and curve of the antique hand-cut mirror set in raised borders of carved and gilded plaster, giving the effect of being inside a huge glittering kaleidoscope.

ABOVE *Viewed from above, an interior courtyard combines the symmetry of traditional gardens with the elegance of tiled water channels and lush vegetation arranged in raised square beds.*

FACING PAGE *Sheltered on four sides by high walls, the central courtyard of the palace is paved with lotus-shaped marble pools lined with marigold-colored mosaic tiles. In the evening, this elegant space is transformed into a delightful open-air dining room lit with thousands of twinkling fairy lights hung on the branches of pomegranate and orange trees.*

FOLLOWING PAGES *The design of the recently constructed turquoise-tiled pool and spa was inspired by traditional Rajput garden pavilions, which incorporate cusped arches and tall windows set with colored glass.*

Recent additions include a two-story Ayurvedic spa and health club designed in Rajput revivalist style, incorporating cusped arches and tall windows set with colored glass. Guests sun themselves on cushioned platforms beside a turquoise-tiled pool while they enjoy a fresh lime soda, roasted almonds, and the famous savory snacks of Jaipur.

Raghvendra Singh, the present rawal of Samode, his younger brother, Yadavendra, and their families live on the top floor of the haveli. They interact regularly with the guests, making sure that the highest standards of traditional Rajput hospitality are maintained. Over the years, Samode Haveli has become a favorite of the chic international set, who treasure its blend of ethnic elegance and the latest creature comforts. Yet it has remained reasonably priced, and a perceptive policy that does not allow large groups adds to the intimate feel of the property.

Umaid Bhawan Palace
JODHPUR

On the edge of the Thar Desert lies Jodhpur, the blue city. It is said that the Hindu Brahmins painted their houses blue to distinguish them from houses owned by others of lower caste. As a result, a magical purple-blue haze hovers above the city.

Located on the caravan route from Central Asia and China, Jodhpur was the ancient capital of the Rathore kingdom, founded in 1459 by Rao Jodha, the Rajput warrior for whom the city is named. In 1839 Jodhpur was forced to accept British control of the region, with Maharaja Takhat Singh as royal figurehead. The prime minister during this time, Sir Pratap Singh, is credited with bringing the first Indian polo team to England, and the special riding breeches worn by his

Indian polo players, known as *jodhpurs*, became popular all over the world.

Perched atop Chittar Hill, amid twenty-six acres of land, stands Umaid Bhawan, an island of creamy pink sandstone in a shimmering sea of sand. This gigantic, three-hundred-and-fifty-room palace, one of Jodhpur's most imposing landmarks, is named after its founder, Maharaja Umaid Singh. In 1925 he traveled to London in search of an architect. He commissioned the Edwardian firm of Lancaster and Lodge to design a new residence in the fashionable art deco style, perhaps because Henry Lancaster was an understudy of Edwin Lutyens, who was instrumental in planning New Delhi. Work began in 1929 at a site dictated by traditional astrological considerations.

PRECEDING PAGES
LEFT *A view of the facade of Umaid Bhawan from the far end of the gardens.*

RIGHT *A view of the grand darbar hall, now the main reception area, from the upper circular gallery. The patterned floor is inlaid with marble.*

ABOVE *This corridor in the private wing of Umaid Bhawan features a French crystal fountain set in a shallow pool.*

RIGHT *The gleaming pink and black bedroom of the maharani is dominated by Stefan Norblin's engraved glass work depicting the powerful goddess Kali riding a black panther.*

Today part of the palace is the residence of Gaj Singh, the grandson of Umaid Singh and the thirty-eighth ruler of the Rathore dynasty. The Marwar Rathores claim descent from Lord Rama and believe they are *suryavanshi*, descendants of the sun god.

Umaid Bhawan, popularly called Chittar Palace by the local public, is a unique example of Indo-Colonial and art deco styles of the 1930s and was the last expression of princely architectural extravagance during British rule. In 1929 widespread famine prompted Maharaja Umaid Singh to put together a famine relief policy that called for several building projects intended to provide work for the local population and to help drought-stricken areas. Included among these projects

BELOW AND FACING PAGE *The maharaja's suite is deco-rated with art deco furniture and painted folding screens by Stefan Norblin. Hung in the sitting area (above) is a portrait of the maharani wearing a sari.*

were Umaid Bhawan and a dam that still works as Jodhpur's main source of water.

The success of this scheme remains questionable among historians. The palace was conceived on monumental scale. More than three thousand artisans worked over fifteen years to build the palace, which was completed in 1944. Massive sandstone boulders were cut from the quarry at Surasagar, eight miles from Jodhpur, and transported by a special narrow-gauge train to the construction sites. Master masons chiseled rough rocks into blocks of five and seven tons. The blocks were then fitted in an interlocking fashion, using no mortar or cement in the construction. The palace is set beneath a cathedral-size dome, measuring one hundred and five feet wide, and arranged in a pattern of ever-increasing concentric circles. The building consumed one million square feet of the finest marble.

Umaid Bhawan first opened as a heritage hotel in 1977. In 2005 the Taj Group leased the palace, and continues to restore and renovate the building. It is undoubtedly one of India's most ostentatious palace hotels.

Rajmahal, the main entrance to the palace, displays the traditional Rathore coat-of-arms, bearing the sacred kite (a bird similar to the crow), an incarnation of the family goddess. As a mark of reverence, kite hunting is not permitted in Jodhpur. The palace contains a private cinema hall, an indoor swimming pool inlaid with tiles depicting the signs of the zodiac, spacious suites, a soaring ballroom, a circular darbar hall, elliptical staircases, marble floors, banquet halls, and teak-paneled libraries. Stefan Norblin, a self-exiled Polish artist living in India, furnished the art deco interiors. Traditional,

locally woven cane screens cool the public rooms; they are doused in cold water to temper the fierce summer breezes that whip off the desert planes. The wings of the building include courtyards and the zenana apartments.

A manicured green lawn stretches out in front of the palace, an unexpected sight in the middle of a desert. The seeds for the grass were imported from Kenya. Two million donkey loads of Indian soil were required to lay out the lawns. Rows of red, orange, pink, purple, and white circular-shaped bougainvillea bushes decorate the gardens and, from time to time, scattering flights of peacocks take to the air. At the far end of the lawn, standing serene, is Bara Dari, a twelve-pillared white marble pleasure pavilion, where musicians entertain the royal family and their guests.

Several festivals and sites of interest can be found in close proximity to the palace. The Marwar Festival is held every year in Jodhpur in the month of Ashwin, between September and October. It lasts for two days during Sharad Poornima (autumn full moon), providing visitors a rare opportunity to see the most talented gypsy dancers and musicians perform dramas portraying Marwar heroes and heroines. A few miles from the palace stands Mehrangarh, a fifteenth-century bastion of palaces, courtyards, and lavishly adorned royal chambers built by Rao Jodha on a vast outcrop of rock. From the vast ramparts, the views of the city's blue-tinted houses and encircling fortifications are breathtaking. Also interesting are the immaculately kept Bishnoi villages, established in the late fifteenth century by Guru Jambhoji, located southeast of Jodhpur. Known for their abiding concern and practice of environmental conservation, Bishnois are staunch believers in the sanctity of life. They hold plants and animals sacred, especially the black buck, also known as the Indian antelope. At Guda Bishnoi, a small lake attracts a wide variety of migratory birds; black buck and chinkaras (Indian gazelle) also gather there.

Lallgarh Palace
BIKANER

The fabled desert kingdom of Bikaner was founded in 1465 by Rao Bika, the fourteenth son of Rao Jodha of Jodhpur. Throughout their long history, the maharajas of Bikaner, responsible for the defense of the borders of Rajasthan from outside invaders, distinguished themselves as great warriors. They also revealed a unique flair for statecraft.

One of the most dynamic and progressive of the twentieth-century princely rulers of India was Maharaja Ganga Singh, born in 1877 inside the magnificent Junagadh Fort, the ancestral palace of the Bikaner royal family. Ganga Singh was only seven years of age when the local British agent decided that the young prince was too deeply influenced by the power politics of the traditional court and the women in the zenana, so he arranged for a new residence to be constructed for him at a considerable distance from the old fort.

The task of designing the new palace was given to Sir Samuel Swinton Jacob, chief engineer of the Jaipur State and a gifted architect attached to the British army. Jacob had already made quite a name for himself with his groundbreaking research into the origins and stylistic development of Rajasthani architecture. Ganga Singh, although still a minor, took considerable interest in the overall concept and decided that it should be named Lallgarh Palace after his father, Maharaja Lall Singh.

A barren stretch of desert five miles away from Junagadh Fort was selected as an auspicious site for the new palace. In 1896, following a ritual blessing of the land, work began in earnest. Jacob based his concept on the traditional Rajput palace, which was arranged around a central courtyard. The four imposing wings of the palace would accommodate both

PRECEDING PAGES
LEFT *Standing at attention, a turbaned doorman complete with ceremonial sword is dwarfed by the magnificent proportions of the carved red sandstone entrance to the Laxmi Niwas wing of the Lallgarh Palace.*

RIGHT *A family of local master carvers created the elaborate floral and geometric motifs that cover every inch of the grand entrance gateway leading into the Laxmi Niwas wing. The ceiling is veneered with thick teakwood panels carved with similar patterns in deep relief.*

ABOVE *A recently refurbished bar opposite the reception desk at Lallgarh Palace boasts a display of antique arms and armor on the walls.*

LEFT *Morning light streams through thin bamboo blinds, covered with colorful cloth, into the sitting area of an upper suite in the Laxmi Niwas wing.*

the private and the ceremonial life of the young maharaja as well as house the female members of the household inside the traditional zenana apartments.

Laxmi Niwas, the grandest of the four wings located on the south side, was the first to be completed in 1902. The imposing entrance gateway is covered with scrolling floral arabesques and geometric patterns carved out of a deep red sandstone, which was quarried locally and used throughout the palace. The interior rooms are arranged around an open arcaded courtyard of grand proportion. The striking façade, which acts as a screen for the zenana apartments behind, is delicately carved with symmetrical rows of *jali* windows articulated by curving eaves and projecting balconies. The stone carvers of Bikaner were famous for being able "to carve stone like butter," and the zenana screen is without doubt their finest masterpiece.

ABOVE *Detail of red sandstone columns carved in deep relief with flower heads and the leafy vegetation of desert plants.*

FACING PAGE *Cooled by an overhead fan suspended from a painted ceiling, the walls of this Laxmi Niwas guest bedroom are intricately carved with jali screens and geometric patterns.*

Although most of the original furnishings are gone, the strong European influence favored by Ganga Singh can still be seen in the marble statuary, crystal chandeliers, and baroque furniture that remain. In a number of principal rooms, however, Western taste merges creatively and successfully with the rich artistic and cultural traditions of Bikaner.

The walls of the Suvarna Mahal, one of the major reception halls, are painted and gilded with foliate patterns and scrolling monsoon clouds inspired directly by the private apartment of the Junagadh Fort, where Ganga Singh was born. Family members were known for their fine marksmanship and their love of hunting, and stuffed animal heads, trophies collected during safaris in India and Africa, hang like relics from another age on the walls of the billiard room. The remaining three wings were built in stages and, by 1926, Lallgarh Palace was completed. A grand celebration was held

inside the soaring darbar hall in the Karni Niwas wing on the north side. This wing also boasts a beautiful art deco indoor swimming pool furnished with white marble benches and illuminated by shafts of light streaming through pastel-colored glass windows.

Converted into a heritage hotel in 1972, Lallgarh Palace is administered by the Maharaja Ganga Singh Trust, which also sponsors many philanthropic and social programs in Bikaner and the surrounding villages. Ably guided by Princess Rajyashree Kumari, the great-granddaughter of Maharaja Ganga Singh, the family trust has been instrumental in saving and preserving much of the recent history of the Bikaner family that would have otherwise been lost. The Sri Sadul Museum has been created inside the west wing of the palace and displays a rich collection of antique photographs, costumes, arms, and armor, as well as family mementos and letters.

PRECEDING PAGES *The painted ceiling in the Laxmi Niwas guest bedroom draws its inspiration from the scrolling patterns of a classical Kashmir shawl.*

ABOVE *Elaborately carved red sandstone columns frame the paved marble arcade leading to the principal reception rooms and suites.*

RIGHT *A panoramic view of the soaring carved red sandstone zenana apartments inside the Laxmi Vilas wing designed by Sir Samuel Swinton Jacob.*

FOLLOWING PAGES *Supported by tall columns, the double-storied swimming pool inside the Karni Niwas wing of the palace is illuminated by art deco windows set with panes of pastel-colored glass and fitted with finely carved white marble benches.*

Princess Rajyashree has fond memories of growing up in Lallgarh Palace: "My childhood was a golden childhood. My brother, sister, and I were blessed with a very intelligent father, Maharaja Karni Singh, who thoroughly spoiled all of us. There were grouse shoots and splendid birthday parties on the palace grounds, and we got to travel on the Bikaner State Saloon, our own private railway car, back and forth to Delhi where my sister and I went to school. We've been able to restore the saloon car just as I remember and it now stands outside the palace. Our aim is to preserve and share our family heritage with all who come, and there's so much more to do. After all, it will even take us a little time to come to terms with more than five centuries of Bikaner history."

Bhanwar Niwas

BIKANER

Located strategically at the crossroads of important trade routes from Central Asia, Bikaner has long attracted large numbers of wealthy merchants and traders, who vied with each other to build the most magnificent residence. Still surviving in Bikaner today are more than a thousand large and small havelis, many of which are kept in good condition by the descendants of the original families who created them.

Among the wealthiest were the Rampurias, a traditional Jain family, whose fortune was founded on the export of cotton fabric to Manchester in the late nineteenth century. Inside the narrow lanes of the old city, which afforded them adequate protection, the Rampuria brothers and uncles constructed five grand mansions, all near to each other. The grandest was built in 1927 by Seth Bhanwarlal Rampuria in a charming blend of neo-Rajput and European styles.

After independence in 1947, and as the demand for cotton began to drop, the Rampurias spent more and more time in Calcutta diversifying the family business into real estate and light industry. Although never completely neglected, Bhanwar Niwas was no longer permanently occupied by the family until 1992, when Sunil Rampuria, a grandson of Seth Bhanwarlal, moved back to Bikaner and converted the ancestral haveli into a heritage hotel, which he opened to the public a year later.

Sunil, a sensitive and thoughtful man who is also a gifted artist, remembers that, although his parents supported his initial plan to convert the property into a hotel, their main concern as strict vegetarians was that no meat should be served on the premises. Ever respectful of family tradition and values, Sunil serves a broad range of delicious continental and local vegetarian dishes in the newly restored grand dining room.

PRECEDING PAPGES
LEFT *This carved column detail from the entrance hallway
is covered with pure gold leaf.*

RIGHT *A confection of European and Rajput styles, the
ground-floor hallway is painted in delicate shades of pink
and mauve with gilded detailing and handcrafted furniture.
The ceramic mosaic floor is set with floral medallions that
lead to the grand staircase at the end of the hall.*

ABOVE *Panels depicting a royal procession and fighting
herons surrounded by stylized Mongol clouds enliven the
walls of one of several grand reception rooms.*

FACING PAGE *Family photographs, gilded figural
lamps, and scrollwork mirrors add to the mix of styles
found in the haveli.*

The walls of this spacious and elegant room have recently been
repainted with elaborate bouquets of flowers arranged in
gilded vases. The work was done by local artists and the owner
himself, who describes the style as "French rococo with a
touch of Bikaner baroque thrown in."

Guests enter the haveli through a carved red sandstone
gateway and are greeted by a liveried doorman standing
proudly beside a vintage 1927 Buick with silver dragon
horns, which had been one of Seth Bhanwarlal's prized pos-
sessions. A series of impressive reception rooms on the
ground floor is sumptuously furnished with Italian marble
fireplaces, gilded European-style furniture, and Bohemian

crystal chandeliers, but the royal heritage of Bikaner is also
well represented. The frescoed walls have been finely painted
and gilded with winged angels, floral arabesques, and tri-
umphant procession scenes inspired by the sublime decoration of the nearby Junagadh Fort, the original seat of the
maharajas of Bikaner.

Restoration and renovation of ancestral properties never
ends, and the owner maintains a small permanent atelier of
some of the most gifted artisans of Bikaner, who repair the old
and create new works of art that decorate this special heritage
hotel, where East meets West with grace and style, just as it
always has.

ABOVE *Two carved and gilded throne chairs stand in front of a grand marble fireplace in one of the public rooms. The painted walls glitter with flowering plants painted in pure gold leaf.*

FACING PAGE *A portrait of Seth Bhanwarlal Rampuria, the founder of the house, stands on the first landing beneath an elaborate staircase carved from imported Italian marble.*

FOLLOWING PAGES *Ancestral portraits, tiled walls and flooring typical of Bikaner, and a massive four-poster bed lend an elegant feel to one of the main bedroom suites.*

LEFT *Carved sandstone railings and white tiled columns festooned with roses frame the corridor running around the first floor just off the dining room.*

ABOVE *An atelier of master artisans continues to work on the restoration of the haveli. The carved and painted marble horse and the geometric gilded mirror behind it were recently created in the workshop.*

Castle Mandawa

MANDAWA

At the heart of the Shekhawati region, a roughly triangular area whose points are Jaipur, Delhi, and Bikaner, lies the remote feudal principality known as Mandawa. It was here that Mandu Jat dug a well, completed in 1740, thereby establishing the *dhani* (hamlet) of Mandawa. Because Mandawa was situated on the caravan route that transported spices, indigo and opium, in 1756 Thakur Nawal Singh built a quadrangular fortress to serve as a halting place for ancient traders from China and the Middle East. During the rule of Nawal Singh's grandsons Padara Singh and Gyan Singh, the building was expanded into a spacious and comfortable residence, with accommodations arranged around a sequence of courtyards. The fortress encouraged traders to settle in the surrounding areas, collectively known as Shekhawati, or Garden of Shekha, named for a local chieftan, Rao Shekha (1433–1488). The

region today comprises three districts in the state of Rajasthan: Jhunjunu, Churu, and Sikar.

Upon entering the bustling town of Mandawa, one sees no sign of the castle or its imposing ramparts. Up a narrow lane, Castle Mandawa rises gradually amid clouds of dust, pot-holed byways, and a muddle of wheezing buses, bullock carts, auto rickshaws, and bicycles. Farther up the lane, visitors encounter enormous iron-spiked wooden gates, big enough for elephants to pass through, and colored flags swirling in the wind above the castle. The gates open into another world, where time seems to stand still. Across the large, sandy courtyard, a maze of verandas and walkways provide meandering passage to the reception and guest rooms. Getting lost and clambering up and down narrow staircases and across rooftop terraces, however, only seem to add to the charm of the experience.

PRECEDING PAGES

PAGE 118 *Detail of a hand-painted arch in the reception area.*

PAGE 119 *The walls in the reception area are adorned with frescoes, portraits, and photographs of members of royal families.*

PAGES 120–21 *A painted ceiling features portraits of royal family members surrounded by floral motifs.*

PAGES 122–23 *Painted archways lead from a reception area into a courtyard.*

LEFT *A bedroom at Castle Mandawa furnished with Anglo-Indian wooden beds.*

ABOVE *View of a marble fountain in one of the bedrooms.*

Castle Mandawa is owned and run by Thakur Kesri Singh, who began restoring the rooms of his eighteenth-century castle in the late 1970s. The owner's sensitive transformation of the building into a hotel, open since 1980, maintains much of the feel of the original castle. Fine murals adorn the exterior and interior walls, and ancestral portraits adorn the darbar,

BELOW *The domed sandstone bar is ideally positioned by the spa and swimming pool.*

RIGHT *The newly built swimming pool, bar, and holistic health spa were designed by architect Amit Ghelot.*

evoking visions of a majestic royal past and curiosity about the people who lived here all those years ago.

Dining at Castle Mandawa is an enchanting candlelit event under the stars, in a large courtyard that can seat at least one hundred guests. The highlight of the evening is the fire dance in which eight men dressed in saffron and red turbans and colorful traditional Rajasthani long coats, called *achkans*, follow an elderly man with a snowy white handlebar moustache. He dances slowly with fire torches in his hands, making circles of flames against the night sky as the procession weaves its way through the courtyard.

Even though Mandawa village declined somewhat after caravan traffic began to dwindle in the late eighteenth century, the region continued to attract wealthy traders called the Marwaris, who built havelis and commissioned local artists to decorate their interior and exterior walls with elaborately painted frescoes. The grand havelis of the Goenkas, Ladias, Sarafs (see page 128, Hotel Mandawa Haveli), and Chokhanias are fine examples of Shekhawati painting and workmanship. Castle Mandawa—reachable via the nearest railway station, in Jhunjunu, about 13 miles (21 kilometers) due southwest— is an ideal base from which to explore the legacy of these eighteenth-century frescoes.

Hotel Mandawa Haveli

MANDAWA

Mandawa is one of several rural hamlets in the Shekhawati region, including Mukundgarh, Nawalgarh, Mahansar, and Bissau, that comprise what has come to be known as a "open-air art gallery." Here lies a concentration of havelis painted inside and out in the distinctive styles of the different hamlets. Because they both built and painted the havelis, the Shekhawati artisans were considered masons as well as *chiteras* (fresco painters) and belonged to the caste of *khumbhar* (potters). Their fresco subjects ranged from epic texts like the *Ramayana* and the *Mahabharata* to historical events and scenes depicting what the merchant owners saw during their travels. These valuable works have withstood the ravages of time and speak volumes about the history of Shekhawati and the habits, beliefs, and aspirations of the peo-

ple living there. As an extension of the royal culture of the region, the havelis also reflected the rich lifestyles of their owners during the mid-nineteenth and twentieth centuries.

In 1890 a prominent Marwari family of jewelers, the Sarafs, built Mandawa Haveli near Sonthaliya Gate, one of the main landmarks of Mandawa, which is adorned with the two *nilgai* (a species of large antelope) of the town's stone-carved crest. In 1986 the Saraf family sold their haveli to Mr. Dhabai, a Rajasthani businessman, and moved to Calcutta. After extensive renovations, Mr. Dhabai reopened the haveli as a heritage hotel in 1999, starting with three guest rooms.

Now known as Hotel Mandawa Haveli, it is one of the last of the havelis whose wall paintings have been left virtually untouched. Their subject is the popular theme of Krishna's

LEFT *This detail of a fresco painted above a carved wooden
beam of a door depicts Krishna and two gopis, a popular
theme.*

RIGHT *Painted walls surround the double-story interior
courtyard.*

ABOVE *Detail of the scalloped arch and painted doorway
at right.*

FACING PAGE *A highly decorated doorway is covered
with scenes from Hindu mythology amid scrolling vines
and floral motifs.*

ABOVE *A guest bedroom, bathed in morning sunlight, features scalloped arches and a painted floor.*

FACING PAGE *Wooden doors lead into a bedroom whose floors have been painted in stripes to resemble the flat woven floor covering known as a dhurrie.*

colorful adventures with the *gopis*. Originally, the painters used only vegetable and natural pigments, such as *kajal* (lamp black) for black, *safeda* (lime) for white, *neel* (indigo) for blue, *harbabhata* (terra verte) for green, *geru* (red stone powder) for red, *kesar* (saffron) for orange, and *pevri* (yellow clay) for yel-

low. At first, the *chiteras* kept to the *fresco buono* technique, in which a small section of the wall was plastered with three layers of very fine clay; the last layer consisted of fine filtered lime dust mixed in limewater, blended into a paste, and plastered onto the walls. The design was drawn and painted while

ABOVE *A wood and brass camel cart with wooden wheels has been transformed into a comfortable bench in the courtyard of the haveli.*

FACING PAGE *In this painted detail in one of the alcoves of the haveli, a Rajput warrior holds a fly whisk, shield, and scabbard.*

the plaster walls were still damp, a situation requiring complete coordination between the painter and the mason. In the last decade of the nineteenth century, as chemical pigments from Germany and England were adopted, the artists could take more time because the new dyes were made to be painted on dry plaster.

The haveli's kitchen specializes in local recipes like *ker-sangri,* a Rajasthani specialty served on *bajra ki roti* (millet bread). Both *sangri* (radish-like pods) and *ker* (long beans) are abundant on bushes and trees that dot the Rajasthani desert. Another key ingredient in local dishes is chickpea flour, used to make delicacies like *khata, gatta ki*

sabzi, and *pakodi.* Another favorite of the haveli is *mangori paapad,* very thin crisp-roasted wafers made from *moong daal* (mung beans).

Today, the previously neglected towns of the Shekhawati region are undergoing a renaissance. Concerned local people have begun to see the potential of their rich heritage and are now getting involved in carefully restoring these heritage properties. This marks a significant change in that, up to now, the conversion of palaces and havelis was solely in the hands of local nobility and wealthy business families from outside the state. Hotel Mandawa Haveli is a successful example of this heartening new trend in heritage conservation.

Khimsar Fort

KHIMSAR

Atrue "diamond in the desert," Khimsar Fort is one of the most exciting and surprising heritage-hotel destinations awaiting a traveler in Rajasthan. The hereditary thakurs of Khimsar trace their descent from Rao Karamsi, who was the eighth son of Rao Jodha of Jodhpur. Rao Karamsi, like his brother, Rao Bika, the founder of Bikaner, left Jodhpur in the mid-fifteenth century to establish his own kingdom. He settled in the desert dunes of Khimsar, 90 miles (145 kilometers) from Jodhpur, and immediately began construction on a mighty fortress surrounded by high stone walls, watchtowers, broad ramparts, and extensive stables for his camels and horses.

For the first hundred years of its existence, Khimsar functioned essentially as a warrior fort, occupied only by the ruler and his army, who were continuously engaged in minor skir-mishes and major battles across the region. Once the political situation was considered safe and stable enough for the thakur's wife and family to settle there, a concentrated build-ing program within the fort began in earnest. A grand palace, with a darbar and a zenana for the ladies of the court were soon constructed, followed by pavilions of pleasure sur-rounded by lush gardens.

The present thakur of Khimsar, Omkar Singh, decided to convert the fort and palace complex into a heritage hotel in 1992. Today his son, Gajendra Singh, who serves as the minis-ter of energy for Rajasthan, and grandson, the twentieth descendant of Rao Karamsi, continue developing this remark-able property. From the beginning, it was decided that guests should experience as closely as possible true Rajput hospitality.

PRECEDING PAGES
PAGE 136 *The magnificent eastern façade of the Khimsar Fort has been recently renovated in traditional Rajasthani style, using projecting balconies, false windows, and domed towers as principal design elements. Thick clusters of fuchsia-colored bougainvillea, which thrive in the dry desert climate, are planted throughout the fort.*

PAGE 137 *Three recently carved sandstone jali windows capped by traditional sloping eaves have been inserted into one of the zenana courtyard walls. Drip irrigation has been successfully installed throughout the fort, enabling a large variety of flowering plants and trees to flourish in the hostile desert environment.*

PAGES 138–39 *The zenana garden courtyard is sheltered by two new wings housing shops and the main dining room, located at the top of the tower block behind colored-glass windows.*

PAGES 140–41 *The doors and windows of the main palace dining room are set with panes of brightly colored glass, resulting in a dazzling display of light and shadow throughout the day.*

RIGHT *Originally part of the zenana apartments, this charming suite, aglow with light falling through jali screens, is one of the oldest and most highly decorated in the palace. The carved arches and walls are painted in shades of green with highlights of pure gold and silver leaf. A bedspread blocked with European-style roses covers the carved double bed.*

FOLLOWING PAGES
The spacious hotel pool is framed by the arched walls of the original fort stables, where the Khimsar camel and horse cavalry were once kept.

As Gajendra Singh has so eloquently put it, "In our heart of hearts, we want everyone who visits to feel that they are part of our family and to get a true feeling of desert life."

Nearly all of the hundred-and-twenty-strong staff at the hotel are recruited locally and trained under the watchful eye of members of the royal family, who try to maintain as closely as possible the traditions and rituals of the Khimsar state. The elegance and refinement of traditional Rajput hospitality are experienced firsthand as guests gather for dinner, served on the broad ramparts of the fort under a star-studded sky. The grand buffet features a variety of Western and Indian dishes, but the real treat is traditional Khimsar royal cuisine, developed in this desert area due to the scarcity of green vegetables, which features a variety of mouthwatering kebabs and delicious meat and wild-game dishes prepared with yogurt, buttermilk, and *ghee*, a form of clarified butter. During the meal, guests are entertained by puppeteers and folk musicians.

Recent additions to the palace complex include a beautifully landscaped swimming pool and spa, two luxurious residential wings, and an exotic mud-brick desert resort nestled in the hollow of sand dunes only a ten-minute drive away. Representing architecture without architects, the additions were designed entirely by Gajendra Singh and his family, who consulted with master stone carvers and masons just as their ancestors did centuries before. Tradition is indeed alive and well at Khimsar Fort.

Kuchaman Fort

KUCHAMAN

The oldest and the highest fortified palace to be converted into a heritage hotel is without doubt Kuchaman Fort, perched on a rocky crag one thousand feet above the white salt flats of Sambhar Lake. Tracing its origins from as far back as the sixth century, when the area was ruled by the Pratihara dynasty, Kuchaman has always been a prize worth fighting for.

Still owned by the royal family of Kuchaman, who established their kingdom here in the early seventeenth century, the long history of the fort and palace are vividly reflected in their magnificent architecture, which has been considerably restored by local artisans during the last ten years. At the base of the mountain, guests enter through a monumental gateway, where they are garlanded with marigolds and greeted with a rather haphazard musical salute played on antique horns and drums. The registration formalities are conducted inside the imposing darbar hall under the watchful gaze of the hereditary rulers of Kuchaman and other legendary heroes of Rajasthan, whose portraits are painted on the domed ceiling above.

In an exciting, but slightly terrifying journey, open jeeps transport guests and their luggage around hairpin turns up the steep and narrow road leading to the main fort and palace complex at the top of the mountain. The view from the broad stone ramparts is spectacular. Kuchaman City is one of the most charming and well laid-out small towns in Rajasthan. The sounds of the bustling bazaar, temple bells, and the Muslim call to prayer all rise upward as falcons and eagles soar above the fort from dawn to dusk.

The portraits are labeled in Devanagari script: दुर्गासिंहजी, रूपलालजी, राबलीयाजी, पाबूराणीद, रावगोगादेव

PRECEDING PAGES
LEFT *One thousand feet above the desert, the fortified walls, palaces, and watchtowers of Kuchaman Fort appear to grow out of the rocky cliff face.*

RIGHT *Glass doors and windows illuminate a multicolored crystal chandelier at the entrance to the main dining room.*

ABOVE *The Diwan-i-am, or Hall of Public Audience, now functions as a reception room for guests. Its walls are painted with images of the hereditary rulers of Kuchaman and other legendary Rajput heroes.*

FACING PAGE *Cloaked by the colorful gilded and painted walls of the Diwan-i-am, rulers would sit on a carved marble throne and conduct the rituals of court.*

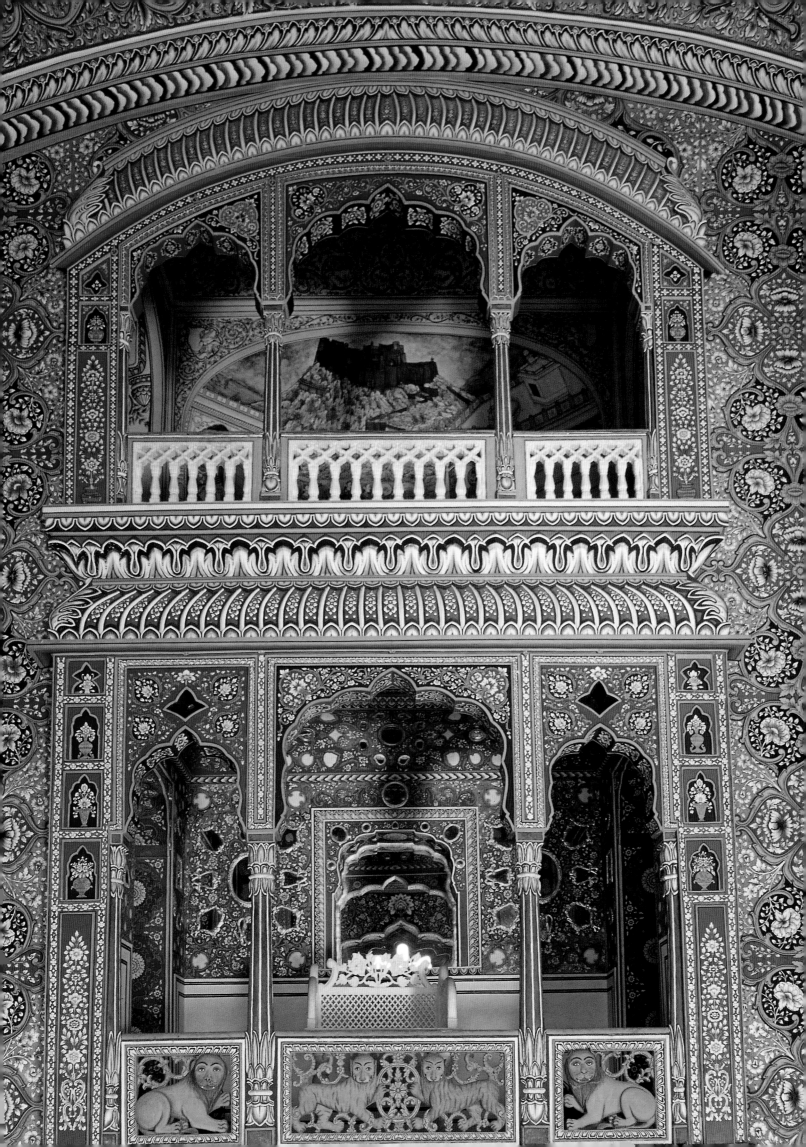

PRECEDING PAGES *Royal portraits of eminent thakurs of Kuchaman, most notably Durgadasji and Raja Zalim Singh, were painted on the domed ceiling of the Diwan-i-am.*

ABOVE *Inverted lotus buds painted in bright colors articulate the arched corners of the dining room.*

FACING PAGE *The original Diwan-i-khas, or Hall of Private Audience, in the upper fort has been successfully converted into the main dining room of the hotel. Since the introduction of air conditioning, quilted fans, once used to cool the guests, now serve primarily as design elements.*

Entry to the main fort is through the elaborately painted Gate of Five Doors, which leads directly into a broad avenue paved with stone and lined on both sides by a raised arcade of small arched rooms. This is the Meena Bazaar, where the ladies of the royal court, traditionally sequestered in the zenana apartments, were able to browse freely and bargain for everything from trinkets to treasure. The long street of the bazaar terminates at the China Gate, a lofty domed vestibule painted in blue and white with scenes of oriental figures, pagodas, and gardens strikingly reminiscent of Ming porcelain. Legend has

it that, nearly three centuries ago, itinerant artists from Central Asia passed through Kuchaman and were commissioned by the maharaja to decorate the China Gate. The exotic style of the paintings, so different from anything else in the fort, suggests that there may just be some truth to the story.

Secret passages, dungeons, step wells, temples, and derelict cannon lie scattered around the fort waiting to be discovered. The hotel swimming pool, known as the Jal Mahal, or Water Palace, was converted from a deep underground chamber originally used to store water in the tenth century in case of siege.

LEFT AND FACING PAGE
Every inch of the Sunehri Burj, or Chamber of Gold, is finely painted and gilded with elaborate floral designs. Along the lower dado (left), a row of handmaidens carrying fly whisks, fans, and other court regalia stand ready to serve the queen of Kuchaman.

FOLLOWING PAGES *Radiant with gold leaf and stone-ground colors, the domed ceiling of the Sunehri Burj is carved in the shape of a full-blown lotus.*

ABOVE AND FACING PAGE *Carved and gilded plaster walls and ceiling, set with thousands of pieces of faceted glass and mirror, create a dazzling effect inside the Sheesh Mahal, or Palace of Mirrors, one of the most beautifully decorated rooms in Rajasthan.*

RIGHT *Viewed through the sculptural forms of the plastered domes of one of the upper palaces, Kuchaman City, one of the most charming small towns in Rajasthan, stretches off into the distance below.*

The real treasure of Kuchaman, however, can be found inside two incredibly beautiful royal apartments at the top of the fort, created in the early eighteenth century especially for the enjoyment of Maharaja Zalim Singh and the ladies of his court. The royal command was given that no cost should be spared and only the greatest of master artisans should be recruited to execute the work. Carved in the shape of a full-blown lotus, the gilded ceiling of the Sunehri Burj, or Chamber of Gold, is embellished with pigments ground from lapis lazuli, malachite, jasper, and other semiprecious stones. Along the lower dado, a frieze of exquisite handmaidens painted in rich tones of red, gold, and amber clearly shows the strong cultural influence of the imperial Mughal court in Agra and Delhi, whose political and diplomatic ties to Kuchaman were very close. With a little persuasion, a padlocked adjoining room can be opened, revealing a gallery of erotic frescoes that even today can titillate and amuse.

A small, narrow staircase leads one floor up to the open courtyard of the Sheesh Mahal, which is paved in marble with a life-size chessboard. It was here that Zalim Singh, seated on a gold and jeweled throne, would move his living chess pieces from square to square. The walls of this extraordinary pleasure pavilion glitter from the reflection of thousands of pieces of faceted mirror set in myriad geometric and floral patterns. Executed in a traditional technique using carved and gilded plaster, scenes of imaginary cityscapes and desert oases filled with minarets and date palms decorate the mirrored walls.

Kuchaman is one of those rare places where, if you close your eyes and listen, you can still conjure up the unabashed pleasures of a royal court who over the centuries clearly perfected the arts of feasting, music, and dance.

Raj Niwas Palace

DHOLPUR

Founded by the Tomar dynasty in the eleventh century, the kingdom of Dholpur, tactically located in the southeastern corner of Rajsthan between Agra and Gwalior, changed hands many times during its long and turbulent history. Looted and occupied by rulers of the Lodi, Sur, and Mughal dynasties, Dholpur was finally absorbed by the British in the early nineteenth century. In 1805, Maharaja Rana Kirat Singh, a local Jat ruler, was placed on the throne.

Raj Niwas, the majestic city palace and present residence of the royal family, was probably constructed sometime in the last quarter of the nineteenth century by Maharaja Nihal Singh. Reflecting the strong political and cultural influence of the British Raj at the time, the imposing two-story palace was built in a neoclassical style out of beige and red sandstone blocks,

which were quarried locally. Dholpur stone had been used for centuries in the construction of Mughal forts and palaces, and the skill of the local carvers was acclaimed throughout the region. Some of their finest work can be seen in the magnificent *jali* windows, carved in a variety of geometric and floral patterns, positioned throughout Raj Niwas, where they continue to filter the gentle movement of light and air.

Descended from a distinguished line of rulers who actively embraced the world of politics, Maharaja Dushyant Singh, also a member of Parliament, decided in 2002 to convert his ancestral palace into a heritage hotel. Working with a team of designers and skilled artisans, he has personally supervised an extensive restoration and renovation program for the palace, which is now nearing completion. The sprawling terraced

RIGHT *Light streams through carved jali screens inside a downstairs reception hall. Upholstered chairs have been arranged around a marble fountain to provide a comfortable seating area for guests.*

gardens and lakes, which once surrounded Raj Niwas as well as the principal reception rooms on the ground floor, have all been restored to their original splendor. Ancestral portraits, Bohemian chandeliers, Italian marble statues, and gilded baroque furniture add a regal old-world charm to these sumptuous rooms. On the first floor, the walls of the principal guest suites and bathrooms are completely veneered with boldly colored tiles imported from England in the early twentieth century, a unique decorative feature found only at Raj Niwas. Even so, old family retainers and staff, overseen by a charming and bubbly housekeeper, lend a touch of home to the grand palace.

There is a lot to do and see in and around Dholpur. Nostalgic for the legendary gardens of Central Asia, the first Mughal emperor, Babur, built his Lotus Garden, the Bagh-i-nilufar, only a few miles away. Guests can enjoy horseback riding in the low hills that encircle the town or go boating on the nearby Chambal River, where a crocodile sanctuary has been established in the hope of saving this endangered creature.

ABOVE *The traditional gaslights in the dressing room of the Yuvraj (Crown Prince) Suite, now rewired, cast a soft glow on the tiled walls and floor.*

FACING PAGE *The nearly twenty-foot-high walls of the Yuvraj Suite on the top floor of the palace are completely veneered with decorative glazed tiles imported from England in the early twentieth century. The recent repainting of the coffered ceiling closely followed the original color scheme. A pierced wooden screen has been placed before the entrance to the tiled bathroom beyond.*

PRECEDING PAGES *Bold rectangular panels of dark brown and green glazed tiles decorate the sober walls of the Maharaja Suite.*

ABOVE *The tiled walls of the Maharani Suite (at right) depict amber-colored carp navigating their way through swirling waves.*

FACING PAGE *Interlocking patterns of glazed tiles, a Persian carpet on the floor, mirrored almirahs (armoires), and antique beds all contribute to the grand decoration of the elegant Maharani Suite.*

At sunset, the smell of incense and the sound of prayer radiate from the hundreds of ancient temples and folk shrines that line the banks of Mach Kund, a small lake sacred to Hindus, just a fifteen-minute drive outside of Dholpur.

Dushyant Singh credits his mother, Maharani Vasundhara Raje Scindia, the current chief minister of Rajasthan, with instilling in him the importance of preserving the rich cultural heritage of India. In a touching tribute to her influence, he is actively involved in founding an institute dedicated to the revival of the stone-carving industry in the Dholpur area. He also works with local women to promote a variety of traditional arts. It's all in a day's work for a "modern" maharaja.

ABOVE *An unusual nineteenth-century enameled bidet takes pride of place in the corner of the Maharaja Suite bathroom.*

FACING PAGE *Each of the principal suites has its own spacious bathroom decorated in different styles. One of the most whimsical is the Lotus Bath, in the Yuvraj Suite, completely veneered with glazed tiles. The original Victorian shower fittings that spray water from every conceivable angle.*

Laxmi Vilas Palace Hotel

BHARATPUR

Floating in fields of brilliant yellow mustard, the Laxmi Vilas Palace Hotel, perched strategically on the old Agra road leading to Jaipur, is the perfect base from which to explore the abundant wildlife, magnificent monuments, and the turbulent history of the kingdom of Bharatpur. Built in 1887 by Rao Raja Raghunath Singh, the younger brother of the erstwhile maharaja of Bharatpur, Ram Singh, this whimsical confection of Rajput and Mughal architecture welcomes visitors through a carved sandstone portal leading to the colorfully painted central courtyard, the heart of the palace. The founder's grandson, Rao Raja Raghuraj Singh, and his elegant wife, Rao Rani Rita Singh, together with their sons, converted their ancestral home into a heritage hotel in 1994 and haven't looked back since. The family still maintains its own residence in one wing of the palace and is actively involved in day-to-day activities.

The charming and spacious rooms are draped with traditional block-printed textiles, and framed photographs of the family celebrating royal weddings and religious festivals adorn the walls. Recent additions include an elegant swimming pool, health club, and spa. Traditional Rajasthani and continental food is served in the columned dining room and central courtyard. Construction has also recently begun just next door for the Shiv Niwas Palace, a sister hotel designed in the grand, traditional Rajput style, which is scheduled for completion in 2008.

PRECEDING PAGES

LEFT *A monumental two-story gateway carved from local beige sandstone leads directly to the central interior courtyard of the palace. A traditional welcome of marigold petals and fresh leaves has been arranged in a floral pattern in front of a marble fountain.*

RIGHT *A carved, painted, and gilded nineteenth-century wooden door marks the entrance to the hotel.*

ABOVE *Painted by local artists on the wall of the outer courtyard, a royal procession, led by a caparisoned elephant, greets visitors to the palace.*

RIGHT *Wall paintings, carved doors and arches, and antique lamps lend an old-world charm to the inner courtyard.*

ABOVE *Lakshmi, the Goddess of Learning, seated on a swan and playing an Indian stringed instrument called a vina, protects and blesses the entrance to Room 115.*

FACING PAGE *Rooms are arranged around a two-story interior courtyard where guests gather for drinks and dinner. A marble fountain in the center, scented with rose water, adds a soothing touch.*

In winter, guests gather in the courtyard around wrought-iron braziers to hear the epic tales of Bharatpur recounted by Rao Raja. The stories begin in the late eighteenth century with the meteoric creation of the Bharatpur state by Maharaja Suraj Mal, an enterprising local Jat leader, who, seeing the weakness of the imperial Mughal power, grabbed large tracts of land for himself. In a series of humiliating raids, his powerful armies looted Delhi and Agra, carrying back to Bharatpur the gates of the Delhi fort and even some of the white marble screens surrounding the tomb of Shah Jahan at the Taj Mahal. Rao Raja, warming to his favorite subject, explains that, over time, the royal states of Rajasthan were gradually absorbed into the British Raj. The Bharatpur rulers were granted a seventeen-gun salute and continued to live in great splendor.

In the early twentieth century, Maharaja Kishan Singh, who was fond of duck shooting, created a nesting and hunting ground out of acres of marshland just outside the town. Visitors from all over the world came, and it was here in 1938 that the British viceroy, Lord Linlithgow, bagged a record number of 4,273 ducks.

Times and values have changed, and in 1964 the marshland was given by Maharaja Vrijendra Singh to the country to form the Keoladeo Ghana National Park, recognized by UNESCO as a world heritage site. Each winter, thousands of migratory birds arrive from the farthest corners of Asia in search of food and a warm place to nest. One of the rarest is the white Siberian crane, who sits serenely on the treetops while spotted cheetah, wild deer, and fourteen-foot-long pythons sun themselves below. Rao Raja concludes, rather wistfully, that, although the old days are gone forever, the rich heritage of Bharatpur remains alive and well and, more than ever, accessible to all who come to visit.

BELOW *Fountain in the entrance courtyard.*

RIGHT *Cooled by paved floors and a marble fountain reminiscent of the one in the entrance courtyard (below), this typical guest room is furnished with block-printed curtains, an antique rocking chair, and a grand four-poster bed.*

FOLLOWING PAGES *The imposing eastern facade of the palace is reflected at dawn in the newly constructed pool and spa.*

Devi Garh Fort Palace

DELWARA

The construction of this soaring yellow sandstone fort and rambling palace complex at Delwara began in the 1760s under Rajput Maharaja Raghudev Singh II. His descendants continued for another hundred years to embellish and expand the central fortress, adding to its architectural splendor and harmony.

Originally known as Fort Delwara, Devi Garh is located about 15 miles (30 kilometers) northeast of Udaipur. Unable to maintain the property, the most recent royal family abandoned the fort in the 1960s and moved to Udaipur. The palace languished for more than twenty years; roof terraces and courtyards decayed and *jharokha* balconies and *chhatri* turrets collapsed. The only signs of life were flocks of lime-green parakeets busily swooping in and out of the crumbling sandstone pavilions.

Today, Devi Garh stands amid jasmine-scented flower gardens, gently rippling fountains and reflecting pools, and a new generation of parakeets, which continue to swoop in and out of the restored shaded pavilions. The towering exterior walls of the building are studded with tiny arched niches, designed by the original architects of the fort to provide ready-made nests and hideaways for coupling parakeets and their chicks. After about ten years of insightful restoration and committed work by designer and new owner Lekha Poddar and talented architects Nareen Gupta, Gautam Bhatia, and Rajiv Saini, the palace welcomed its first guests in 2001. It was Lekha Poddar who renamed the palace Devi Garh (Fort of the Goddess).

PRECEDING PAGES

PAGE 184 *The sandstone fort rises amid lush flowering plants and leafy trees.*

PAGE 185 *Beyond a scalloped archway, giant iron-spiked wooden gates open into the main courtyard of the fort.*

PAGES 186–87 *The original darbar hall of the fort, where visitors were welcomed and entertained by the maharaja, today serves as a large public room for guests. It is decorated minimally, with ivory-white walls, sleek saffron-colored sofas, and cane screens.*

PAGES 188–89 *Arches within arches, ornamented with mirror work, colored glass, and ceramic tiles, lead from one room to another.*

RIGHT *A game room is framed by scalloped arches of white marble and furnished with contemporary tables and chairs.*

The restored exterior is entirely traditional, evoking both the dreamy opulence of its Rajput past and a modern spirit of simple lines, which brings it into the twenty-first century. All over the building are inviting places to sit and relax, whether in the open air or in a shady alcove. At night these become ideal locations for stargazing. There are never-ending courtyards within courtyards, and the deeper you venture inside them, the more you encounter opportunities for finding yourself outside. The idea, it seems, was to construct an alcove so secluded that it was entirely exterior. Guest rooms are clustered around a series of courtyards reached via a network of corridors and steep, wide stone stairs. Large strides have to be taken to cover one stair. A giant stylized sculpture of Ganesh (Remover of Obstacles) stands in an alcove at the top of one staircase. Unusual textures and patterns hidden in niches and on walls are offset by marigold silks and flashes of gold and silver.

The palace's large organic vegetable garden provides healthy greens for the guests. Dishes might include *bhindi* (okra), Hyderabadi *murg avadhi korma* (chicken cooked Hyderabad style), *dal makhni* (simmered lentils with butter), and *gajar ka halwa* (sweet carrot pudding). Local village women are invited to lead interested guests through the intricacies of the Indian bread repertoire of *chapati, naan, paratha, rumali roti, puri,* and more. Guests can also float in the dark green marble swimming pool or try one of the eighteen Ayurvedic treatments.

ABOVE *Fragrant rose petals float in a scalloped white marble bowl.*

RIGHT *In the Silver Room, tables and chairs have been ornamented in silver and complemented by shades of silver and gray raw-silk fabrics. Architectural details include mirror work and carved sand-stone arches and columns.*

ABOVE *This portion of a hand-painted mural depicts Lord Shiva wearing a turban made from a coiled serpent.*

RIGHT *The white dining room at Devi Garh is enlivened by the painted mural at the far end of the room.*

ABOVE *A rooftop terrace, with pavers ornamented by abstract grass designs, provides a view of the Aravalli hills and verdant countryside in the month of November.*

RIGHT *In one of the many courtyards of the fort, a stone water fountain features at its center an ancient sandstone segment of a pillar, carved with figures of Hindu gods.*

ABOVE *A closer view of the* chhatri, *showing the scalloped arches of the pavilion.*

RIGHT *A black-bottomed marble pool and shaded* chhatri *overlook the Aravalli hills in the distance.*

The rooftop terraces provide sweeping views of a seemingly idyllic rural life. The village of Delwara is an authentic agricultural hamlet that has not changed much since it was founded four hundred and fifty years ago. The month is November; everything is fertile and abundant, unlike the parched surroundings in the hot summer months. Among emerald green fields, goats and cows graze in the sun. People gather at an ancient stone step well in the middle of the village to catch up on the latest news, bathe, and wash their clothes, as they have done for centuries. Walking distance from the palace fort is the group of fourteenth-century Jain temples that formed the inspiration for the famous temples of Dilwara near Mount Abu. Eklingji, a sandstone and marble temple to Shiva that dates back to 734 A.D., lies about three miles away.

Deogarh Mahal

DEOGARH

Deogarh (Fort of the Gods) Mahal is reached by way of a very narrow, dusty street containing a bustling bazaar with colorful shops, roadside shrines, animals, bicycles, and people everywhere. The chaos gradually subsides as a cobbled street winds uphill, through enormous wooden and iron gates, into a large central courtyard. The dazzling yellow-ocher domes, *chhatri* towers, and *jharokha* balconies, set off by ivory-white trim, overlook the small village of Deogarh below.

Located in the Mewar region between Ajmer and Udaipur, Deogarh is one of the most remote of the heritage hotels. A wooded principality surrounded by beautiful countryside, hills, and lakes interwoven into the rugged desert landscape, it is the seat of the Chundawat clan of Sisodia Rajputs. The absence of a substantial middle class in rural Mewar means

that the old families, especially the local rulers, called rawats, are as prominent today as they have always been. As the royal family's jeeps proceed through the narrow streets of the bazaar, almost all the older inhabitants of the village shower them with blessings.

Deogarh is owned and run by Veerbhadra Singh Chundawat and his brother Shatrunjai. Their father, Rawat Nahar Singh, is a retired history professor from Mayo College (founded in 1875 by Lord Mayo in Ajmer), where most of the Rajput princes continue to be educated. A few years ago, Rawat Nahar Singh noticed that the fort was beginning to fall apart and made a gift of the palace to his eldest son, who returned from planting tea and coffee in the south to restore the rambling building.

PRECEDING PAGES

PAGES 200–1 *The entrance is flanked with paintings of ceremonially adorned horses. Carved-stone figures stand guard beside the steps.*

PAGES 202–3 *In the Sheesh Mahal (Palace of Mirrors), small disks of mirrors cover the walls, pillars, and ceiling. Sunlight streaming through the colored-glass windows bathes the room in sparkling light.*

ABOVE *This guest room features a red velvet chauper set. Chauper is a traditional four-player game, similar to Parcheesi, that can be traced back to the fourth century in India. The game is played using lacquered dome-shaped wooden pieces and cowrie shells.*

FACING PAGE *Diffused light filters into a bedroom suite through a green and yellow beaded curtain.*

PRECEDING PAGES *A raised-platform sitting area within an arched alcove provides a private place for resting or reading.*

ABOVE *Wall detail of a carved and painted flower.*

FACING PAGE *This charming alcove features scalloped arches, colored-glass windows, and carved and painted columns and walls*

The stately gateway into the front courtyard passes beneath the *kacheri* (public court) of powerful rawats of Deogarh. The ornately painted palace entrance leads past two small family shrines, through a series of narrow passages, and up a well-worn staircase to the general administration area, where in earlier times villagers came to pay their feudal dues or to seek some judicial remedy. Beyond and above is the private section of the palace, built on three levels arranged around an upper courtyard, which is now the hotel.

Originally built by Rawat Gokal Dasji in 1670, Deogarh Mahal was designed by the Sompura family of architects, who specialized in the traditional art of temple architecture based on the *Vastu Shastra*, an ancient treatise on design and building that incorporates science, art, astronomy, and astrology. In transforming this ancestral home into a heritage hotel, the owners took great care to retain the integrity of its original style. The rooms are furnished with traditional textiles, faded sepia family photographs, painted royal portraits, and elaborately mirrored and frescoed walls. With names like Keseria Mahal (Saffron Palace), Kasumal (Magenta) Mahal, and Mayoor (Peacock) Mahal, all sixty rooms, including a number of elegant royal suites, are reflections of an ancient opulent era, each with its own historic tale to tell.

ABOVE *Ceiling detail showing a carved and painted rosette and a Belgian glass chandelier.*

FACING PAGE *This bedroom suite is highlighted by a colored-glass window and a carved sandstone frieze.*

Seengh Sagar

DEOGARH

Three miles outside Deogarh, via an exhilarating jeep ride on a dirt road through rocky terrain, past a *dargah* (shrine of a Muslim saint) and the ruins of the deserted village of Manpura, lies Seengh Sagar, a small island fortress that seems to grow organically out of the rocks. The rawats of Deogarh ruled over about two hundred area villages, and the only way to control their large domain was by having small forts spread throughout the territory. Seengh Sagar is one such fort.

Built in 1806 as a fortified hunting lodge, Seengh Sagar is surrounded by a small lake teeming with bird life, bordered by the Aravalli hills. Depending on the monsoon rains, the fort can be reached by boat or by car crossing a small bridge. It has been admirably restored with four exquisite suites, with each

room opening onto the central courtyard. Delicious Rajasthani cuisine is prepared in the traditional kitchen.

Seengh Sagar is a unique and memorable oasis from which to explore the surrounding countryside. Not far from Deogarh is Kumbhalgarh, built in the fifteenth century by Maharana Khumba. Enclosed within Kumbhalgarh are 360 temples. The fort's perimeter walls extend 18 miles (approximately 36 kilometers) and are said to be the longest in the world after the Great Wall of China. The amazing Jain temple in nearby Ranakpur appears to be in constant motion due to the way the stone architecture has been carved and constructed in uneven layers. It features 1,444 hand-carved white marble pillars, no two of which are alike.

PRECEDING PAGES
LEFT *The corner watchtower of the fort overlooks the surrounding landscape.*

RIGHT *An ornately carved sandstone doorway leads into the courtyard.*

LEFT *Bathed in gentle morning sunlight, the central interior courtyard contains seating for al fresco dining.*

ABOVE *In the indoor dining room, tables are set with Rajasthani thalis (traditional large silver plate and bowls). The dining room opens onto the central courtyard through scalloped arches.*

ABOVE *A double-pillowed seat is upholstered with block-printed fabric and detailed with satin.*

RIGHT *A recessed circle in the floor of one of the bedroom suites holds a carved fountain of polished yellow sandstone.*

FOLLOWING PAGES *The family owners have taken meticulous care to furnish the suites with locally handcrafted furniture and textiles.*

ABOVE *A bathtub is adorned with green and blue marble-mosaic tile. Local rocks embedded into the wall give the en suite bathroom a rustic outdoor look.*

RIGHT *A rooftop terrace with woven cane and coir-fiber chairs looks out on the surrounding lake, the rugged desert landscape, and the Aravalli hills in the distance.*

ABOVE *An outdoor rooftop dining area provides serene views of the lake.*

RIGHT *A comfortable seating area is an ideal spot for watching the birds and animals that border the shores of the lake at sunrise and sunset.*

Taj Lake Palace

UDAIPUR

Awhirring water taxi glides through the smooth waters of Lake Pichola, with breathtaking views of Udaipur's City Palace behind and the gleaming white Taj Lake Palace floating ahead. *Gangaur,* the palace's antique, ceremonial, turquoise-blue barge with red sails, passes with guests who want to experience a royal boat ride. On the far side of the lake, cut into the hillside, is Sajjangarh, the Monsoon Fort, where Mewar royals, known as the Sisodias, retreated during the rainy season. To the left is the small, floating Jag Mandir, the original pleasure palace of the Sisodia rulers and famous for providing refuge to Prince Khurram (the future emperor Shah Jahan) from his father, Emperor Jehangir, during their family power struggles.

Originally known as Jag Niwas, the Taj Lake Palace covers the whole of Jag Niwas Island and is built on a natural foundation of four acres of rock. Maharana Jagat Singh II, a great patron of the arts, built the palace in 1746 as a summer retreat. It is said that, as a young man, he resented his father's refusal to allow him to have moonlit picnics with the ladies of his zenana on the neighboring island palace, Jag Mandir. Thus, as soon as he assumed the throne, Jagat Singh II commissioned the construction of Jag Niwas. The original village of Pichola was submerged under water and the lake artificially enlarged to provide extra protection to the royal family against invading armies. Jagat Singh admired Mughal emperor Shah Jahan and encouraged his craftsmen to use the building techniques

PRECEDING PAGES
LEFT *With its gleaming white chhatris reflected in the water, the Taj Lake Palace appears to float serenely on Lake Pichola.*

RIGHT *Mughal-style architecture encloses a shaded garden courtyard with a lotus water fountain of white marble and polished yellow sandstone.*

LEFT AND ABOVE *An interior lounge with ornamented arches invites guests to read or play board games.*

FOLLOWING PAGES *Guests can dine outdoors on a rooftop terrace surrounded by sweeping views of Lake Pichola and the vast City Palace buildings on the opposite side.*

employed to construct the shah's magnificent Taj Mahal in Agra. The palace faces east so that residents can pray to the rising sun. During Jagat Singh's reign, he completed the Bara Mahal (Large Palace), Phool Mahal (Flower Palace), and Khush Mahal (Palace of Happiness), which accommodated the Sisodia queens. Here in this ideal setting, the Mewar rulers enjoyed courtly entertainment, boating parties, picnics, and musical performances. It remained their summer residence for two hundred years.

By the latter half of the nineteenth century, time and weather had taken their toll on Jag Niwas, popularly known as the lake palace. The palace remained in disrepair until Bhagwat Singh ascended the throne in 1955. The new ruler struggled with many inherited problems, however. Not only was he faced with the task of restoring numerous deteriorating royal properties, but he also had to determine what to do with three hundred dancing girls and the twelve state elephants that had belonged to his predecessor, Maharana Bhopal Singh.

ABOVE *Small arched porthole-style windows look out onto the lake from a bedroom suite furnished with raised silk-upholstered banquettes and plush cushions.*

FACING PAGE *Originally the apartments of the Sisodia maharanis, the Khush Mahal (Chamber of Happiness) is tucked away in the rear of the palace. An antique swing is suspended by decorative brass chains, and a wall of jalis partitions the room. The floor has been inlaid with polished yellow sandstone and white marble.*

He decided that the only way to preserve Jag Niwas's heritage was to turn it into a luxury palace hotel. Under the supervision of design consultant Didi Contractor, an American artist, pavilions were enlarged, and ponds and gardens were cleaned and repaved. Also uncovered were many unusual features of the palace that had been hidden for years, including peepholes, secret passageways and chambers, and a room that could be entered only through a trap door at the top. In 1963 Jag Niwas opened as the Taj Lake Palace and quickly became a popular destination for celebrities around the world.

A second restoration program was begun in 2000. Singapore-based architects and designers carefully researched Mewar architecture and building types, as well as historic artifacts and local crafts from the region, in order to preserve and restore the original elements of the architecture and design of the interiors. Today, lily ponds and rippling fountains ornament interior courtyards. Spacious rooftop terraces and marble pavilions invite guests to sit at sunset and gaze at the golden-tipped waves lapping against the building. In the evenings, the notes of a flute reverberate through the corridors as a musician sits cross-legged, playing in one of the many alcoves. Wonderful views of Mughal-style architectural details abound: projecting balconies and white marble *jalis* and *chhatris* are interspersed with flowering crimson bougainvillea. Jag Niwas's heritage remains, and the Taj Lake Palace is once again a true floating pleasure palace.

PRECEDING PAGES *In this magical view of Khush Mahal, jalis paneled with colored glass transform the sun's rays into a kaleidoscope of flickering color, shadows, and light.*

ABOVE *A mural inlaid with mirrors depicts an ornately dressed royal couple and a female attendant. A parakeet perches on the prince's finger, and the princess holds peacock feathers. The attendant carries a mirror under her arm.*

RIGHT *The lily pond in the large central courtyard of the palace is edged with whimsical stone-carved Mughal floral motifs. Manicured green hedges and champa trees contribute to the lush environment.*

Shiv Niwas Palace

UDAIPUR

I n 1556, after losing Chittorgarh, his fortress capital, to Mughal Emperor Akbar, Mewar Maharana Udai Singh founded a new capital, which he named Udaipur (city of Udai), after himself. Part of a line of rulers who considered themselves the founders of the Rajput dynasty, the Mewars, also known as the Sisodias, preferred the title rana (warrior) rather than raja (king). Over the centuries, the Mewar maharanas (great rulers), many of them noted warriors, builders, administrators, and poets, developed Udaipur's lavish City Palace complex.

On the edge of Lake Pichola, set high among the towers and cupolas of the City Palace, is Shiv Niwas, a royal penthouse begun under the rule of Maharana Sajjan Singh (1874–1884) and completed by his successor, Maharana Fateh Singh. At first intended as a royal guesthouse, the palace displays a royal crest inscribed with the words *atithi devo bhava* ("treat a guest as if he or she were God").

Formally part of the City Palace complex, Shiv Niwas was constructed as a progression of buildings on three levels, arranged in a grand crescent-shaped arc from which sixteen ornately furnished suites open onto an oval interior courtyard and marble swimming pool. The buildings reflect both Rajput and European architectural traditions. The maharana sent two of his master court artisans, Khaja Ustadh and Kundan Lal, to England to learn the arts of glass-mosaic design and European fresco painting. Thus, although the high exterior stone walls are stark and undecorated in the Rajput manner, the walls inside are embellished with magnificent paintings, frescoes, marble and colored-glass inlay, and mosaics.

LEFT *A semicircular veranda overlooks the interior courtyard
and swimming pool as well as palace suites across the way.*

RIGHT *A grand gateway, with a large brass-studded wooden door,
leads into the main courtyard. Greenery tumbles over the head of a
stone elephant, which projects out of a side wall.*

LEFT *A portrait of Maharana Pratap Singh (1572–1597) dominates what
was originally the darbar hall, where maharanas once entertained guests.
The high-ceilinged room has been transformed into the Paneera Bar.*

ABOVE *The teak door leading into the Paneera Bar is intricately inlaid
with old ivory in a scrolling floral design. The use and sale of ivory has
been illegal in India since 1972.*

ABOVE *An outdoor dining room situated on a rooftop terrace affords spectacular views of Lake Pichola and the Aravalli hills.*

FACING PAGE *A large marble swimming pool occupies the interior courtyard of the palace.*

FOLLOWING PAGES *Scalloped arches frame the view from a rooftop pavilion.*

In 1982, Maharana Bhagwat Singh opened Shiv Niwas as a hotel, and the palace continues to be developed by the present representative of the Sisodia family, Arvind Singh Mewar. Shiv Niwas now contains thirty-one guest rooms and suites that have been modernized and refurbished by interior designer Elizabeth Kerkar. The elaborate furnishings and ornament include ivory and mother-of-pearl inlay work, crystal glass, carefully chosen Persian carpets, and gleaming white marble. Each room has its own ornate *jharokha* balconies and *jali* windows, from which guests can absorb extensive views of shimmering Lake Pichola, bordered by the soaring Aravalli hills, the Taj Lake Palace, and Jag Mandir.

Nature enthusiasts and bird-watchers will find the western shores of Lake Pichola a paradise. Boats are available to ferry guests to nesting sites where many migratory bird species can be observed. The Vintage and Classic Car Collection, housed in the original Palace Garage, showcases old limousines and rare automobiles belonging to the House of Mewar, all in perfect running condition.

In addition to being custodian of the entire City Palace complex, Shri Arvind Singh is an environmental and cultural conservationist who oversees the Maharana of Mewar Charitable Foundation (MMCF). HH, as he is fondly known, harbors an ambition to convert Udaipur into India's first "solar" city; to that end, he has developed a fleet of solar-powered auto rickshaws, motorcycles, and boats.

Udaivilas

UDAIPUR

It is Kartik Poornima, the full moon in the month of Kartik, and the beginning of Sharad, the season of autumn. The November skies are a clear turquoise blue. The tuneful cries of birds and the sounds of gently rippling fountains fill the air as orange-red dragonflies hover and dart inches above lotus ponds. Here in the verdant Girwa Valley, not quite concealed behind green foliage, appear the salmon-colored domes of Udaivilas, a structure as unique as it is impressive. Rightly called a Rajasthani palace for the twenty-first century, Udaivilas is not a renovation but has been built from scratch. Ideally situated on the shores of Lake Pichola, directly across from the maharana's palace, it serves as a tribute to Udaipur's greatest living artisans.

The work of Oberoi Group, Udaivilas opened its doors in August 2002, twenty years after the developers' first tentative discussions with the ruling Sisodia family and ten years after construction began. Modeled on authentic Mewari palaces, the building's carefully planned design has evolved as a seamless assimilation of spaces resembling the original model: a network of courtyards and corridors interspersed with pools and fountains, sandstone pavilions and rooftop terraces. Udaivilas also encompasses thirty acres of landscaped gardens designed by Bill Bensley. Within these former royal hunting grounds stands Bara Mahal, an original Mewari hunting lodge now two hundred and fifty years old.

PRECEDING PAGES
LEFT *A scalloped archway frames a view of sand-colored domes and rooftop terraces.*

RIGHT *A carved white marble elephant and rider guard the entrance, and crystal-clear reflecting pools border the palace buildings.*

ABOVE *Detail of a canopied dining area.*

RIGHT *Seen from one of the many rooftop terraces, the large domes of the palace and an outdoor dining veranda overlook the serene waters of Lake Pichola and the white city of Udaipur in the distance.*

FOLLOWING PAGES
PAGES 252–53 *A gold-leaf-patterned dome interior and a Belgian glass chandelier add grandeur to one of the public guest rooms of the palace.*

PAGES 254–55 *Even in the daytime, the play of light and shadow adds drama to the Candle Room. The patterned marble floor frames the central table and its collection of gilded candle stands and candles.*

ABOVE *An S-shaped chair for two looks out into a small garden alcove.*

FACING PAGE *The main entrance into the palace is embellished with a huge gilded dome, a Belgian glass chandelier, and a white marble water fountain.*

LEFT *A bedroom suite with a private terrace is furnished with raw silks and the finest cottons, as well as dark wood furniture and Rajput miniature paintings.*

ABOVE *Diffused light streams into an alcove through fine-cane blinds. The sitting area is stacked with a dazzling array of silk, cotton, and mirrored cushions.*

ABOVE *Flowing water in the central courtyard's large pond is fragmented by stylized lotus flowers and leaves carved out of pure white marble.*

FACING PAGE *Sweeping views from a rooftop terrace reveal the vast central courtyard and entrance gateway beyond. The lawn and pond in the central quadrangle are bordered by black and white steps.*

The eighty-seven suites are spacious havens of comfort that look out onto gardens and walled courtyards. Some rooms overlook Lake Pichola; others offer views of the wildlife sanctuary that is home to spotted deer and strutting peacocks. Many rooms overlook infinity pools that meander past each terrace. Water cascades over marble fountains, carved to resemble fish scales in the silver sunlight. Every turn brings surprise and discovery.

Master craftspeople scoured old manuscripts for the secrets of the Mewari builders in order to re-create the wonders of the past, such as the elaborate mirror-mosaic work called *thekri*.

An ancient Rajasthani technique, *thekri* is made when molten glass is blown into circular balls using pipettes; after the balls have cooled, molten metals are poured onto them, coating their concave sides. The balls are then broken into concave shards, shaped, and applied in different patterns to the surface of the dome, using a mixture of lime and marble powder as adhesive. In the Candle Room, a domed sanctuary holds a central table filled with a myriad of gilded candlesticks. At night, the amber light of the candles reflects the dome's *thekri* ornamentation, which required one million, seventy-five thousand mirror pieces and thirty-five days to complete.

Udaivilas represents an idealized India, freed from the realities of history. At Udaivilas there are no historical layers of peeling paint; instead, the walls have been finished with *ghutai*, a secret mix of stones ground and blended with egg white and tamarind to create a soft ivory finish that shines with the luminosity of satin. Curving under a grand marble staircase is a large freshly painted fresco of mountains and lakes, tigers and birds, mango trees and flowering plants. The artist, Mohan Singh Kumawat, used the traditional fresco pigments of ground stone mixed with tree-bark resin.

The two restaurants at Udaivilas serve international, North Indian, and Rajasthani cuisine. In the Indian restaurant, Udaimahal, menus have been carefully chosen after many hours of research in traditional Rajasthani kitchens. For some, however, a salad of organically grown arugula with warm goat's cheese and aged balsamic vinegar can be a welcome change of pace.

Housed within a large bi-level domed building painted with exquisite birds flying across a wide expanse of blue sky, the spa offers the best in Ayurvedic, Thai, and Balinese massage and aromatherapy. An in-house Ayurvedic physician is also available for consultation. Many who arrive at Udaivilas are reluctant to leave, especially after discovering the spa.

DIRECTORY OF PRINCELY PALACE HOTELS

Listed below are the hotels included in the book, as well as a few additional hotels that may be of interest to the reader.

ALSISAR HAVELI
Sansar Chandra Road
District Jaipur
Jaipur, Rajasthan 302 001
Tel: 91 (0)141 2368 290 / 2364 685
Fax: 91 (0)141 2364652
E-mail: alsisar@alsisar.com
Web: www.alsisar.com

BHANWAR NIWAS
Rampuria Street
District Bikaner
Bikaner, Rajasthan 334 005
Tel: 91 (0)151 2529323 / 2201043
Fax: 91 (0)151 2200880
E-mail: bhanwarniwas@rediffmail.com
Web: www.bhanwarniwas.com

CASTLE MANDAWA
District Jhunjhunu
Mandawa, Rajasthan
Tel: 91 (0)159 2223124 / 2223432
Fax: 91 (0)159 2223171
E-mail: reservations@castlemandawa.com
Web: www.castlemandawa.com

DEOGARH MAHAL
Deogarh Madaria
District Rajsamand
Deogarh, Rajasthan 313 331
Tel: 91 (0)2904 252777
Fax: 91 (0)2904 253333
E-mail: info@deogarhmahal.com
Web: www.deogarhmahal.com

DEVI GARH FORT PALACE
District Rajsamand
Village Delwara, Rajasthan 313 001
Tel: 91 (0)2953 289211-20
Fax: 91 (0)2953 289357
E-mail: devigarh@deviresorts.com
Web: www.deviresorts.com

FORT RAJWADA
Jodhpur-Barmer Link Road
District Jaisalmer
Jaisalmer, Rajasthan 345 001
Tel: 91 (0)2992 253233 / 253533
Fax: 91 (0)2992 253733
E-mail: sales@fortrajwada.com
Web: www.fortrajwada.com

HOTEL MANDAWA HAVELI
Near Sonthaliya Gate Madawa
District Jhunjhunu
Mandawa, Rajasthan 333 704
Tel: 91 (0)1592 223088
Fax: 91 (0)1592 224060
E-mail: hotelmandawahaveli@yahoo.com
Web: http://hotelmandawa.free.fr

THE IMPERIAL
Janpath
New Delhi 110 001
Tel: 91 (0)11 23341234 / 41501234
Fax: 91 (0)11 23342255
E-mail: luxury@theimperialindia.com
Web: www.theimperialindia.com

KHIMSAR FORT
District Nagaur
Khimsar, Rajasthan 341 025
Tel: 91 (0)1585 262345-9
Fax: 91 (0)1585 262228
E-mail: khimsar_jp1@sancharnet.in
Web: www.khimsar.com

KUCHAMAN FORT
District Nagaur
Kuchaman, Rajasthan 341 508
Tel: 91 (0)1586 220884
Fax: 91 (0)1586 220882
E-mail: sales@kuchamanfort.com
Web: www.kuchamanfort.com

LALLGARH PALACE
Dr. Karni Singhji Road
District Bikaner
Bikaner, Rajasthan 334 001
Tel: 91 (0)151 2540201-7
Fax: 91 (0)151 2523963
E-mail: info@lallgarhpalace.com
Web: www.lallgarhpalace.com

LAXMI NIWAS PALACE
Dr. Karni Singhji Road
District Bikaner
Bikaner, Rajasthan 334 001
Tel: 91 (0)151 2202777 / 2521188
Fax: 91 (0)151 2521487
E-mail: reservation@laxminiwaspalace.com
Web: www.laxminiwaspalace.com

LAXMI VILAS PALACE HOTEL

Kakaji Kothi, Old Agra Road
District Bharatpur
Bharatpur, Rajasthan 321 001
Tel: 91 (0)5644 223523 / 231199
Fax: 91 (0)5644 225259
E-mail: reservations@laxmivilas.com
Web: www.laxmivilas.com

NARAIN NIWAS PALACE

Kanota Bagh, Narain Singh Road
District Jaipur
Jaipur, Rajasthan 302 004
Tel: 91 (0)141 2561291 / 2563448
Fax: 91 (0)141 2561045
E-mail: kanota@sancharnet.in
Web: www.narainniwas.com

NEEMRANA FORT-PALACE

District Alwar
Village Neemrana, Rajasthan 301 705
Tel: 91 (0)1494 246006-8
Fax: 91 (0)1494 246005
E-mail: sales@neemranahotels.com
Web: www.neemranahotels.com

PHOOL MAHAL PALACE

District Kishangarh
Kishangarh, Rajasthan 305 802
Tel: 91 (0)1463 247405 / 247505
Fax: 91 (0)1463 247505
E-mail: phoolmahalpalace@yahoo.com
Web: www.royalkishangarh.com

RAJ NIWAS PALACE

District Dholpur
Dholpur, Rajasthan
Tel: 91 (0)5642 220216
Mob: 91 (0)9414027979
Fax: 91 (0)5642 221271
E-mail: info@dholpurpalace.com
Web: www.dholpurpalace.com

RAMBAGH PALACE

Bhawani Singh Road
District Jaipur
Jaipur, Rajasthan 302 005
Tel: 91 (0)141 2211919
Fax: 91 (0)141 2385098
E-mail: rambagh.jaipur@tajhotels.com
Web: www.tajhotels.com

SAMODE HAVELI

Gangapole
District Jaipur
Jaipur, Rajasthan 302 002
Tel: 91 (0)141 2632407 / 2632370
Fax: 91 (0)141 2631397
E-mail: reservations@samode.com
Web: www.samode.com

SAMODE PALACE AND SAMODE BAGH

District Jaipur
Samode Town, Rajasthan 303 806
Tel: 91 (0)1423 240014 / 240023
Fax: 91 (0)141 2632370 / 2631397
E-mail: reservations@samode.com
Web: www.samode.com

SEENGH SAGAR

Deogarh Madaria
District Rajsamand
Deogarh, Rajasthan 313 331
Tel: 91 (0)2904 252777
Fax: 91 (0)2904 253333
E-mail: info@deogarhmahal.com
Web: www.deogarhmahal.com

SHIV NIWAS PALACE

The City Palace Complex
District Udaipur
Udaipur, Rajasthan 313 001
Tel: 91 (0)294 2528016-19
Fax: 91 (0)284 2528006 / 2528012
E-mail: crs@udaipur.hrhindia.com
Web: www.hrhindia.com

TAJ LAKE PALACE

Pichola Lake
P.O. Box No. 5
District Udaipur
Udaipur, Rajasthan 313 001
Tel: 91 (0)294 2528800
Fax: 91 (0)294 2528700
E-mail: lakepalace.udaipur@tajhotels.com
Web: www.tajhotels.com

UDAI KOTHI

Hanuman Ghat
Udaipur, Rajasthan 313 001
Tel: 91 (0)294 2432810-12
Fax: 91 (0)294 2430412
E-mail: udaikothi@yahoo.com
Web: www.udaikothi.com

UDAIVILAS

Haridasji ki Magri
District Udaipur
Udaipur, Rajasthan 313 001
Tel: 91 (0)294 2433300
Fax: 91 (0)294 2433200
E-mail: reservations@oberoi-udaivilas.com
Web: www.oberoihotels.com

UMAID BHAWAN PALACE

District Jodhpur
Jodhpur, Rajasthan 342 006
Tel: 91 (0)291 2510101-5
Fax: 91 (0)291 2510100
E-mail: ubpresv.jodh@tajhotels.com
Web: www.tajhotels.com

SELECTED BIBLIOGRAPHY

Allen, Charles, and Sharada Dwivedi. *Lives of Indian Princes*. London: Century Publishing, in association with the Taj Hotel Group, 1984.

Badhwar, Inderjit, and Susan Leong. *Indiachic*. Singapore: Bolding Books, 2006.

Barnard, Nicholas, and Robyn Beeche. *Arts and Crafts of India*. London: Conran Octopus, 1994.

Barrett, Matt. *Footprint Rajasthan*. Bristol: Footprint Books, 2005.

Basham, A. L. *The Wonder That Was India*. London: Fontana, 1971.

Beach, Milo Cleveland. *Mughal and Rajput Painting*. Cambridge, 1992.

Beny, Roloff, and Sylvia Matheson. *Rajasthan*. London: Frederick Muller Limited, 1984.

Cimino, Rosa Maria. *Life at Court in Rajasthan*. Florence, 1985.

———. *Wall Paintings of Rajasthan: Amber and Jaipur*. New Delhi: Aryan Books International, 2001.

Crill, Rosemary. *Marwar Painting: A History of Jodhpur Style*. New Delhi, 1999.

Davies, Philip. *The Penguin Guide to the Monuments of India*. Vol. 2, *Islamic, Rajput, European*. London: Penguin Group, 1989.

Drew, Joanna, ed. *The Living Arts of India*. London: Arts Council of Great Britain, 1982.

Everyman Guides: *Rajasthan*. London, 1996.

Fass, Virginia. *The Palaces of India*. New York, 1980.

Faucon, Regis, and Sophie Regis. *Palais-Hotels du Rajasthan*. Paris: Editions Acanthe, 2005.

Garde, Anne, and Sylvie Raulet. *Maharajas' Palaces: European Style in Imperial India*. London, 1997.

Gascoigne, Bamber. *The Great Moghuls*. London: Jonathan Cape, 1971.

Gayatri Devi and Santha Rama Rau. *A Princess Remembers*. Philadelphia: Lippincott, 1976.

Goetz, Hermann. *The Art and Architecture of Bikaner State*. Oxford, 1950.

Gotswami, Shrivatsa. *Celebrating Krishna*. Vrindavan: Sri Caitanya Prema Samsthana, 2001.

Gupta, M. L. *Frescoes and Wall Paintings of Rajasthan*. Jaipur, 1965.

Hooja, Rima. *A History of Rajasthan*. New Delhi: Rupa & Co., 2006.

The Indian Heritage: Court Life and Arts Under Mughal Rule. Exhibition catalogue. London: Victoria and Albert Museum, 1982.

Jacob, Sir Samuel Swinton. *The Jeypore Portfolio of Architectural Details*. 12 vols. London, 1890–1913.

Jain, Shikha. *Havelis: A Living Tradition of Rajasthan*. New Delhi: Shubhi Publications, 2004.

Jaitly, Jaya. *The Craft Traditions of India*. London: Tiger Books International, 1990.

Livingston, Morna. *Steps to Water: The Ancient Stepwells of India*. New York: Princeton Architectural Press, 2002.

Manchanda, Bindu. *Forts and Palaces of India: Sentinels of History*. New Delhi: Roli Books, 2006.

Michell, George. *The Penguin Guide to the Monuments of India*. Vol. 1, *Buddhist, Jain, Hindu*. London: Penguin Group, 1989.

Michell, George, and Antonio Martinelli. *The Royal Palaces of India*. London: Thames and Hudson, 1994.

Moynihan, Elizabeth. *Paradise as a Garden in Persia and Mughal India*. New York, 1979.

Nath, Aman. *Jaipur: The Last Destination*. London: Tauris Parke Books, 1996.

Nath, Aman, and Francis Wacziarg. *Arts and Crafts of Rajasthan*. New York: Mapin International Inc., 1987.

Nicholson, Louise. *India in Luxury: A Practical Guide for the Discerning Traveller*. London: Century Hutchinson Ltd., 1985.

Piper, Jon, and George Michell, eds. *The Impulse to Adorn: Studies in Traditional Indian Architecture*. Bombay: Marg Publications, 1982.

Rakesh, P., and K. Lewis. *Shekhawati: Rajasthan's Painted Homes*. Delhi, 1995.

Randhawa, T. S. *The Indian Courtyard House*. New Delhi: Prakash Books, 1999.

Robinson, Andrew. *Maharajas: The Spectacular Heritage of Princely India*. London: Thames and Hudson, 1988.

Sharma, M. L. *History of the Jaipur State*. Jaipur, 1969.

Singh, Chandramani. *Protected Monuments of Rajasthan*. Jaipur: Jawahar Kala Kendra, 2002.

———, ed. *Wall Paintings of Rajasthan*. Jaipur: Jawahar Kala Kendra, 1998.

Sugich, Michael. *Palaces of India: A Traveller's Companion Featuring the Palace Hotels*. London: Pavilion Books Ltd., 1992.

Tadgell, Christopher. *The History of Architecture in India*. London, 1990.

Tod, James. *Annals and Antiquities of Rajasthan*. 3 vols. London: Ed. W. Crooke, 1920.

Thapar, Romila. *Early India: From the Origins to AD 1300*. Berkeley: University of California Press, 2003.

Thomas, P. *Festivals and Holidays of India*. Bombay: D. B. Taraporevala Sons & Co. Private Ltd, 1971.

Tillotson, Giles. *Jaipur Nama: Tales from the Pink City*. New Delhi: Penguin Books, 2006.

———. *The Rajput Palaces: The Development of an Architectural Style, 1450–1750*. Bombay, Calcutta, Madras: Oxford University Press, 1987.

Topsfield, A. *An Introduction to Indian Court Painting*. London, 1984.

Wacziarg, F., and Aman Nath. *Rajasthan: The Painted Walls of Shekhawati*. London, 1982.

Welch, Stuart Cary. *India: Art and Culture 1300–1900*. New York: The Metropolian Museum of Art, 1986.

Welch, Stuart Cary, and Naveen Patnaik. *A Second Paradise: Indian Courtly Life, 1590–1947*. London, 1985.

Welch, Stuart Cary, and Milo Cleveland Beach. *Gods, Thrones and Peacocks*. New York: The Asia Society, 1976.

Zimmer, H. *Myths and Symbols in Indian Art and Civilization*. New York, 1946.

ACKNOWLEDGMENTS

First and foremost, we wish to thank the current owners and hoteliers who allowed us to photograph and include their restored historic properties in this book. They are the current stewards of India's rich cultural, artistic, and historical heritage. It is due to their commitment, care, and foresight that this heritage continues to evolve in innovative and inspiring ways. We would also like to thank the original owners, as well as the all the original architects, landscape architects, artists, and builders, long deceased, who first constructed and over the years embellished these palaces, forts, and havelis. Their imagination, building skills, and artistic techniques are a testament to the enduring appeal of these buildings, which continue to amaze, inspire, and surprise at every turn.

Additional thanks go to a number of individuals who generously gave their time, assistance, and advice. They are Caroline Desouza of Saray Gallery, Ketaki Narain of The Oberoi Group, Princess Rajyashree of Bikaner, Aman Nath, Francois Wacziarg and Peter Dessa of Laxmi Niwas Palace, Bikaner.

Thank you to Hugh Levick for his constant patience, good nature, and support. Thank you to Anne Laval for her generous spirit and supportive presence. Thank you to Niloufar Afshar-Crites for her warm hospitality in India. In Paris we would like to thank Didier Sandman and his wonderful agency, La Route Des Indes, for getting us started on the right track, and Granon Photo for their excellent work in processing our film. Thank you to Antonio Martinelli for his visual inspiration and useful advice.

This book would not have been possible without the guidance, wisdom and skills of the editorial, design and production team at Rizzoli. In alphabetical order, Gerrit Albertson, Douglas Curran, Maria Pia Gramaglia, Kaija Markoe, David Morton, Abigail Sturges, and Harriet Whelchel. Thank you to Charles Miers for his immense enthusiasm and encouragement. Finally, we are very grateful to our agent, Sarah Jane Freymann, for her commitment and dedication.

We would also like to give a special thanks and acknowledgment to Gita Bhalla and Devika Surie at the Equinox Travel Agency in New Delhi, who meticulously planned and coordinated our journeys across Rajasthan. Their patient support through our many and frequent trip changes contributed greatly to the success of the book.

INDEX